#1 INTERNATIONAL BEST SELLER

INSPIRING STORIES AND STRATEGIES FOR WOMEN IN BUSINESS

SHE BUILT IT!

Angela Sedran | Rachel WingMan | Jenny Godfrey | Michelle Huntington
Heather Disher | Polina Kesov | Jo Cooper | Sophie Firmager
Cristina Santangelo | Sue-Ann Wilson | Suzanne Rath

Copyright
By **Angela Sedran**, Rachel WingMan, Jenny Godfrey, Michelle Huntington, Heather Disher, Polina Kesov, Jo Cooper, Sophie Firmager, Cristina Santangelo, Sue-Ann Wilson, Suzanne Rath

© Copyright 2024
All rights reserved.
Book Layout ©2024

Evolve Global Publishing
www.EvolveGlobalPublishing.com

No part of this book may be reproduced or transmitted in any form or by any means, electronic or mechanical, including photocopying, recording or by any information storage and retrieval system, without written permission from the authors, except for the inclusion of brief quotations in a review.

Limit of Liability Disclaimer:
The information provided in this book is for informational purposes only and is not intended to be a source of direct consulting with respect to the material presented. The information and/or documents contained in this book do not constitute legal or financial advice and should never be used without first consulting a qualified advisor to determine which strategies may best fit your individual needs and be customized to your unique situation.

The publisher and the authors do not make any guarantee or other promise as to any results that may be obtained from using the content in this book. Meeting with a qualified advisor and conducting your own research and due diligence is always recommended. To the maximum extent permitted by law, the publisher and the authors disclaim any and all liability in the event any information, commentary, analysis, opinions, advice and/or recommendations contained in this book prove to be inaccurate, incomplete, unreliable, or result in any type of loss.

Content contained or made available through this book is not intended to constitute legal advice or financial advice, and no attorney-client relationship is formed through this published work

Earnings Disclaimer: All income examples in this book are examples. They are not intended to represent or guarantee that everyone will achieve the same results. You understand that each individual's success will be determined by his or her desire, dedication, background, effort, and motivation to work. There is no guarantee you will duplicate any of the results stated here. You recognize any business endeavours have inherent risk or loss of capital.

She Built It! Inspiring Strategies and Stories for Women in Business

1st Edition. 2024 v3.3
ASIN: B0D1YMQLNC (Amazon Kindle)
ISBN: 978-1-923223-31-8 (eBook)
ISBN: 978-1-923223-32-5 (Amazon Paperback)
ISBN: 978-1-923223-33-2 (Amazon Hardcover)
ISBN: 978-1-923223-34-9 (Ingram Spark Paperback)
ISBN: 978-1-923223-35-6 (Ingram Spark Hardcover)
ISBN: 978-1-923223-31-8 (Smashwords)

CONTACT THE PUBLISHER
Business Name: Evolve Global Publishing
Website: www.evolveglobalpublishing.com

TRADEMARKS
All product names, logos, and brands are the property of their respective owners. All company, product, and service names used in this book are for identification purposes only. Using these names, logos, and brands does not imply endorsement. All other trademarks cited herein are the property of their respective owners

CONTENTS

Introduction vii

Dedication xi

Acknowledgements xiii

About the Authors 1

About the Author: Angela Sedran 4

Chapter 1: From Tragedy to Triumph: A Woman's Journey to Success 5

About the Author: Rachel WingMan. 18

Chapter 2: Gratitude in Motion: Rachel WingMan's Journey from Adversity to Empowerment 19

About the Author: Jenny Godfrey 36

Chapter 3: Raising a (family) Business 37

About the Author: Michelle Huntington 56

Chapter 4: Flying Solo Across the Pacific. 57

About the Author: Heather Disher. 72

Chapter 5: My Leadership Journey 73

About the Author: Polina Kesov. 86

Chapter 6: Unstoppable Resilience: My Journey of Courage. . . .87

About the Author: Jo Cooper 100

Chapter 7: The Good Warrior: Fighting for Justice and Equality. 101

About the Author: Sophie Firmager 114

Chapter 8: The Makings of a Diamond: A Journey of Self-Discovery and Actualization. 115

About the Author: Cristina Santangelo 130

Chapter 9: Beauty in the World of Prettiness 131

About the Author: Sue-Ann Wilson 144

Chapter 10: The Path To Finding Myself: Embracing the joy in taking a leap of faith to create pivotal moments in life. 145

About the Author: Suzanne Rath 158

Chapter 11: Thriving From the Inside Out. 159

Epilogue. 171

Glossary. 175

Index. 185

INTRODUCTION

Welcome to "She Built It: Stories and Strategies for Women in Business." This book celebrates the incredible journeys of women who have not only dreamed big but have also turned those dreams into reality. These stories of women have inspired me profoundly, and I am honoured to share their experiences with you.

In these pages, you will meet Michelle Huntington, the airline captain who refused to accept the notion that women cannot fly, breaking through the clouds and barriers with equal fervour. You will encounter Polina Kesov who encountered sceptics who doubted her ability to succeed as a woman in business after losing her partner to illness. Her journey demonstrates that challenges can become opportunities for growth and success.

You'll read about Heather Disher, who overcame a near-death experience caused by bullying, transforming her pain into a life on her terms. She went on to build two incredible businesses, embodying resilience and strength.

This book also features Jo Cooper, who believes we all have a duty to speak out against injustice. Her courageous stand in the Supreme Court led to a landmark ruling, reminding us of the power of our voices. Sue-Ann Wilson's inspiring story is of a woman who has transformed her family's life through embracing leaps of faith which can be daunting to fuel our passions and create meaningful impact whilst leading a life that is personally purposeful.

You will meet Suzanne Rath, who constantly pushed herself to physical limits and took her health for granted until a devastating biking accident literally stopped her face-first in her tracks. Her journey of recovery inspired her to build holistic health clinics and become a fervent health advocate, turning a personal tragedy into a beacon of hope for others.

You'll also find stories of women who moved to Australia at a very young age and went on to build incredible careers that now inspire and help people live their best lives. Rachel WingMan, The Triple Happiness Coach, took a disfiguring skin condition and turned it into a beauty and wellness empire. Sophie Firmager harnessed her feminine energy to transform adversity into a successful corporate career at Tiffany, only to decide she needed to help more people, leading her to start her own business. There's Jenny Godfrey, who turned her incredible life experiences into a marketing powerhouse.

There's also the story of Cristina Santangelo, who pursued a corporate career to prove her worth, only to realise one day that it made her miserable and would never prove her worth because worth had nothing to do with it. Discovering the power within herself, she pivoted to a successful career helping other women shine, embodying the transformative power of self-realisation.

Finally, there is my story, the tale of a sole parent who became so after losing her son's father in a car hijacking. Ignoring the advice of law enforcement authorities who told me it was not only impossible but too dangerous, I tracked down an online scammer halfway across the world using nothing but my laptop, reclaiming every cent of the $100,000 stolen from me, plus $20,000 in interest! My journey proves that we are capable of anything when we get out of our own way and trust in our inner strength and determination.

Each story is a testament to the strength, resilience, and ingenuity of women who have faced adversity head-on and emerged victorious. These women come from various industries and backgrounds, yet they all share a common thread: an unwavering belief in themselves and their abilities.

As you read through their narratives, you'll find practical strategies, heartfelt advice, and inspiring anecdotes that will resonate with anyone who has ever faced obstacles in their professional journey. These stories are not just about success; they are about perseverance, determination, and the unyielding spirit of women who refuse to be defined by societal expectations.

My hope is that "She Built It" will serve as both a source of inspiration and a practical guide for women who are building their paths in the world of business. Whether you're just starting your journey or are well on your way, may these stories empower you to believe in yourself, push through challenges, and achieve your dreams.

Thank you for joining us on this journey. Let's celebrate these remarkable women and, in doing so, inspire the next generation of trailblazers.

With admiration, love and hope,

Angela Sedran

DEDICATION

To all women with a dream. Believe in yourself.
We already do.

ACKNOWLEDGEMENTS

Creating this book has been a journey of inspiration and discovery, and it would not have been possible without the incredible support and encouragement of many people.

To the remarkable women whose stories fill these pages, thank you for sharing your journeys of resilience, strength, and success. Your experiences have profoundly inspired me, and I am honoured to share them with the world.

To my family and friends, your unwavering belief in me has been my anchor. To my son, who is my greatest motivation, thank you for being my guiding light.

A special thank you to all the mentors, colleagues, and readers who have supported and believed in this project. Your encouragement has been invaluable.

Together, we celebrate the strength of women and the power of dreams.

With gratitude and admiration,

Angela Sedran

ABOUT THE AUTHORS

Angela Sedran
Strategy Execution and Authentic Leadership Thought Leader, Professional Speaker and Bestselling Author

Rachel WingMan
Triple Happiness Coach

Jenny Godfrey
Mum, Digital Marketing Strategist and Author

Michelle Huntington
Inspirational Keynote Speaker, Leadership Coach, Podcast Host, Corporate Trainer, and Media Commentator

Heather Disher
Multifaceted Business Owner with Energy and Heart

Polina Kesov
Drawing from Personal Adversity to Offer Unmatched Support and Guidance to Business Owners

Jo Cooper
Warrior for Change

Sophie Firmager
Entrepreneur & Author

Cristina Santangelo
Inclusive Image Consultant & Style Coach

Sue-Ann Wilson
Taking leaps of faith to define your authentic life: Sue-Ann Wilson's purpose.

Suzanne Rath
Coach and Speaker

Angela Sedran
Strategy Execution and
Authentic Leadership Thought Leader,
Professional Speaker and Bestselling Author

ABOUT THE AUTHOR: ANGELA SEDRAN

Angela Sedran teaches ambitious business owners and leaders how to master leadership and business growth strategies, even if they currently feel stuck or lack a clear roadmap.

Angela is an Italian and Australian management consultant, executive coach, author, anddynamic professional speaker. This book represents her third collaboration, a testament to her unwavering commitment to empowering individuals.

Angela holds a Bachelor of Commerce (Hons) and an MBA from the prestigious Australian Graduate School of Management, showcasing her dedication to education and excellence. Her pursuit of excellence is exemplified by her business, The Business Growth Accelerator, which has been acknowledged with numerous awards. Her personal mission is to help a million women globally achieve financial freedom by 2030.

As an industry thought leader, seasoned management consultant, and executive coach, Angela is a respected member of the Australian Institute of Company Directors and ICF. She is also a proud member of the Forbes Coaches Council and an Executive Contributor to Brainz Magazine.

With over 15 years of strategic advisory experience, Angela has guided businesses to the top 2% of national revenues, scaling ventures into multi-million-dollar enterprises. However, her clients will tell you it's not just about financial success; it's about becoming authentic leaders destined for greatness.

Beyond her professional achievements, Angela is a devoted single mother, rarely seen without her beloved Malshi companion, Mia. Fluent in five languages, she's an intrepid adventurer, animal lover, globe-trotter, and creative spirit. Her adventures span from tobogganing down the world's largest sand dunes to camel treks in the desert, thrilling white-water rafting, glacier climbs, New Zealand motorbike journeys, quad biking, scuba diving, jungle treks above the Iguazu Falls, and even tango dancing in Buenos Aires. One of her proudest moments remains achieving something the FBI deemed impossible.

CHAPTER 1

FROM TRAGEDY TO TRIUMPH: A WOMAN'S JOURNEY TO SUCCESS

By Angela Sedran

I grew up in Apartheid South Africa, the only child of a strict, temperamental Italian father and a German mother. I attended a liberal private Catholic convent with friends from diverse ethnic backgrounds. Occasionally, there were conflicts between the girls, and I was the one people turned to for help resolving them.

My outings were limited to visiting a friend's house or going to the movies. I was very competitive and always strived for top marks. I particularly enjoyed history, French, public speaking, and debating. Some of my friends asked me to tutor them so they wouldn't fail, and one of them joked that I was the reason she made it through high school. Overall, I was a model student and considered a good girl.

My dad put me on my first diet when I was 9. I was teased at school. I don't remember being teased at all, but I do remember being on a constant diet in my teens. By the time I was 15, I was taking handfuls of laxatives, appetite suppressants, and diuretics.

My father, in a misguided attempt to help, would monitor what I ate and was constantly pushing me to go to the gym. I felt ugly and worthless because I certainly couldn't match up to my dad's ideal of what a woman should look like.

I was fortunate to spend several Augusts in Italy with my nonna, my father's mother. It felt like being released from prison for both of us, and we cherished every moment. Unlike my Oma, my nonna wasn't a warm and cuddly grandmother, but when she passed away, I realised that she, in a way, filled the role that a sister would have. When we travelled as a family, it was always the two of us sharing the backseat of the car or a hotel room. Some of my fondest and happiest childhood memories were in Italy with her and my dad's cousins.

I love design, architecture, and animals, so I wanted to become an architect or a vet. My father had other plans, so whilst my friends went off to university, I spent my first year after school at home writing my A-levels so I could apply to a foreign university. Then my dad decided it was too dangerous for me to go to university on a campus like all my friends, so he decided I was to undertake a BCom via correspondence.

My life after school suddenly shrunk to the point where I only got to leave the house to go to the shops. So, at a time when I should be going out in the world and discovering who I was, I suddenly became a prisoner of my own home. And I was miserable.

My mother had a market research business and worked from home. Her typist moved cities, so I suggested using this new thing called the "internet" to keep working with her typist. We needed someone with tech skills to help set that up, so I walked my son's father.

He was in his mid-thirties with an established career, and we fell madly in love. In hindsight, I think I was blinded by the fact that I thought this was my ticket to freedom and that a man loved me and made me feel worthy.

We decided that the quickest way to be together was to become a family, so I fell pregnant. I was terrified to tell my parents, who were old school. My mother had always told me that they would throw me out of the house if I ever came home pregnant. Instead of throwing me out, they pressured me every day to give my child up for adoption.

It was one of the saddest, most traumatic few months of my life. All I knew was that I wanted to keep my baby. And I did. It was only after they saw him on Christmas Day in the neonatal unit that my mother told me to bring him home. I was still under 21, so I couldn't live with my son's dad.

The bottom fell out of my world a few months after my son was born when my son's dad was killed on the way to work in a car hijacking. Whilst this type of horrific crime was a daily occurrence in South Africa, no one ever thought something like this would happen to them - until it did.

So, if I had been trapped before, I was now more trapped than ever. My world fell apart as I came to terms with being a young mother with very low earning potential raising a son on her own. I was halfway through an accounting degree when I found myself solely responsible for myself and my little person. It wasn't easy, but I made it work with the money I earned through a part-time job in market research while finishing my degree and living with my parents.

Mandela's new government took over in 1994. Everyone was joyous and optimistic about the new rainbow nation South Africa had become. But the crime rate kept rising, and the currency continued to devalue, making it harder and harder for people to survive - literally and figuratively. We constantly lived in fear of being kidnapped, raped, or murdered - or all three.

My biggest fear was being hijacked and having my car taken with my son still strapped in the back. This had happened to many others, and eventually, it became clear to me that we had to leave South Africa because it was just too dangerous.

That move to Australia in 1997 involved my mom, my nonna, my son, and me, accompanied by our ten dogs. My dad was stuck in a management buyout and followed full-time two years later. I was determined to build a good life for myself and my son. The problem was that Australia is expensive. Nursery school then cost $1,200 a month, and my salary was only $3,000.

So, determined to elevate our future, I embarked on an MBA. The journey was intense, and I'm indebted to my parents for supporting my son. Commitment isn't just about saying 'yes'; it's about facing every challenge and finding ways to persevere. In a class where only 28% were women, I stood tall, proud to be among those breaking barriers.

Halfway through my second year, my son was seriously falling behind the other kids at school because it turned out that he was technically deaf owing to the multiple ear infections he was plagued with from a very young age. This caused the progressive loss of his hearing to the point where he could only sense sound through the bone rather than the eardrum, and, to compensate, he taught himself to lip-read.

Life's curveballs can sometimes throw us off, but I've realised it's all about bouncing back. It's about sifting through those experiences, finding the little gems – the lessons, the memories, the growth – and cherishing them. Even when things don't go as planned, there's always something valuable we can take away.

Fortunately, the doctor managed to restore his hearing surgically, but by that time, my son had missed out on almost four years of being able to hear in his early pre and primary school years. The learning and development he'd missed out on during that period couldn't be restored overnight. He needed years of expensive remedial teaching. This wasn't cheap, but I was committed to doing whatever it took to give him the best opportunities I could.

My role was in strategy with PBL, then part of James Packer's group. For the next 14 years, I threw myself into my corporate career, focusing on earning as much as possible to give my boy all the help he needed. I was determined to do everything to ensure he would achieve his dream of becoming an engineer. And he did. I feel like I'm the proudest mother ever because of the beautiful young man my son has become.

I enjoyed my work. Working with PBL's Hoyts group and travelling to India to negotiate a joint venture with DLF, one of the world's biggest property developers was a highlight. There was only so much that could and needed to be done to grow PBL's business strategically, and I thrived at the challenge.

My next role was Strategy Director at LexisNexis, one of the world's two biggest legal publishing firms. The business was going through a massive change. Paid legal publishing was dying, given that much of the law was published free on the internet, so the business started buying legal practice management software.

My role was to delve into various research assignments, help the company manage the change, and re-engage its people.

I had an internal office on the executive level with a big glass window, won which I used to write quotes in colour marker pens. Staff from across all seven floors would visit my office, telling me it was a breath of fresh air. I attended corporate strategy conferences in New York and Paris and travelled to places like London and Boca Raton to research strategy papers.

As hard as I tried, I was never completely happy in corporate life. Spending the day making money for giant corporations failed to light my fire. I also hated the politics of corporate culture. There always seemed to be something disingenuous and unauthentic about it, so being retrenched during the GFC was a blessing.

So, here I was in a depressed job market with very little savings. I started two businesses in the time it took to find another job. One involved making candles; the other was an online women's sensuality boutique. My candles sold well, but it took a lot of work to make them, and they were difficult to transport because the jars they were housed in were glass.

My online boutique also proved popular, but an e-store like that involves having stock, which ties up a lot of cash. To grow, I needed an equity partner and a business coach. I didn't know how to find either. These businesses taught me that we don't know what we don't know. And for my part, I didn't know how to raise funds to grow my businesses.

Then, I started an in-room romance kit for the hospitality industry. I secured a contract with the Star Casino. We imported bespoke bottles of massage oil from California, bespoke poker chips that said "your choice" on one side and "my choice" on the other, blindfolds made in Thailand and a few other bits and pieces.

These experiences were a turning point in my life in that I learned that I could survive on my own and that I didn't need my father's approval, and my confidence grew.

It took me 18 months, but eventually, I found a job and retreated to the 'safety' of the corporate world and a regular income because I still believed that I wasn't good enough to be successful working for myself.

This time, I ventured into consulting, which was a fantastic experience! I worked with different businesses, providing them with consultation, coaching, training, and facilitation. I loved it! We had big clients like BHP Billiton and George Weston, which was exciting.

I realised that my years of psychology research not only helped me overcome my struggles with low self-esteem and an eating disorder but also allowed me to help my clients develop their leadership skills. It was so fulfilling to help businesses achieve their vision finally.

My biggest client was a subsidiary of BHP Billiton. It was a $750k annual contract, and I delivered year after year. The CEO loved me, and the staff loved me. I ran their entire strategy execution program, which included nearly 14 workshops a year, and I organised their annual conference.

My life was going well. I had a steady job as a management consultant and executive coach and married again in 2012. I had reservations as I walked down the aisle but felt committed and beyond the point of no return.

I finally felt reasonably secure because I had a dependable job and a man I thought loved me in my life. However, in the five years we spent together, my husband was trying to develop his idea into a new business, which meant I was the full-time breadwinner.

I worked my full-time job and a side hustle, looking after my husband and stepdaughter. I'd come home from work, and the house would be messy with dishes piled high in the sink. I'd come home from work, clean, and work until midnight.

We had each other's back, though - or so I thought!

A medical investigation in 2015 around the reason I'd lost my sense of taste led to the discovery of a lesion on my brain. Then, I found out that my husband was having an affair. The kicker was that he spent more money on his friend in three weeks than on me during our entire relationship.

I remember confronting him. With utter disgust for me on his face in his eyes, he said, "You are such a selfish bitch! You could be dying of a brain tumour. All I am doing is trying to find a replacement wife, and you are denying me that!" And that was that. I duly thanked him and immediately cut him out of my life. Saying that was the nicest thing he'd ever done for me because it gave me absolute clarity on what I had to do next.

The following year was beautiful. I focussed on rebuilding my life, starting with putting a plan in place to pay off the sexually-transmitted debt my husband had given me. The plan involved opening a new limited-time zero-interest credit card and rolling over the balance, using the money I saved on interest to pay off the debt.

Before too long, I was back in the black regarding my finances and health because I'd made a concerted effort to look after myself. I was enjoying my independence and felt empowered. The only problem was that I got the shock of my life three days before Christmas 2015 when I logged into my bank account to check if I'd been paid.

Instead, I found that somebody amazed my credit cards out to nearly $100k. This set my life on a whole other trajectory. (And no—I didn't wind up starting a business helping people who've been scammed out of their life savings.)

In terms of getting help, the FBI, the Met and the Australian Federal Police told me to give up, but I didn't – because I felt I had nothing left to lose. And in July 2016, I found a website that mentioned the name of the "company" involved in this scam. I'll never know why, but I shared my story, and within an hour, I received an anonymous tip outlining who the perpetrator was: an Israeli named Shir Gad-el.

This was a common Israeli scam, not illegal in Israel, but it quickly became an embarrassment to the Israeli government. My source provided a screengrab of Gad-el's Facebook page and some background information. Gad-el had spent time in South America and spoke a bit of Spanish. The photo was of a fat, hairy, smug man smoking a cigar and lying on a pink pool flamingo floating on a pool. The last piece of information was an email address.

First, I contacted the Times of Israel, a reporter named Simona Weinglass. Then I contacted my new friend, Shir Gad-el. I told him I would be in Tel Aviv the following week to start civil proceedings against him and that I was talking to the Times. Also, if he didn't refund me immediately, I would set Interpol on him. I knew where he lived and that I had a detective watching him. "Don't believe me?" I told him, "Then how come I know you have a pool and pink pool flamingo and that you speak Spanish?" He replied within 2 hours, and the refunds started flowing back in.

It took a month of nagging to get them all back, but I got them. He told me that he had never been so depressed as when he met me. I assured him that the feeling was mutual. A friend who worked in high-level security warned me off multiple times and told me that I had no idea who I was dealing with. These people could be organised crime. They had taken $100k off me, and it apparently only cost $20k to put a contract on someone. Maybe I was stupid, but I didn't care. I was standing up for myself, and that was that. I also insisted he pay back the credit card interest of 22%. And he did. Although the Times of Israel was ready to publish, I asked Simona not to because I felt I had pushed my luck far enough. I didn't need the potential mob on my back.

This all happened in August 2016, a month I will never forget. At the same time as I recovered my stolen money, my divorce came through, and I negotiated a retrenchment.

I thought to myself, "To hell with it! I am going to work for the best boss in the world—me!" And I did. This time, I went into business fortified by pure passion, emanating from the realisation that I care deeply about helping individuals run their businesses more effectively.

My business vision is to empower a million business owners globally by 2030, equipping them with the right systems and leadership skills to connect on a deeper, more engaging level. By fostering effective business practices and strong leadership, I aim to help entrepreneurs achieve their dreams faster and more confidently.

I am passionate about this mission because I understand the challenges of navigating the business world and the transformative power of effective systems and leadership. By guiding business owners to operate more efficiently and lead purposefully, I aspire to create a ripple effect that enhances productivity, fosters innovation, and drives success across various industries.

This vision is not just about improving business operations; it's about helping individuals realise their full potential and achieve their dreams. Through my clients, I am committed to creating a world where businesses thrive, leaders inspire, and communities benefit from the positive impact of well-run enterprises.

Today, I empower business owners to scale their businesses with the right operating systems and leadership. With my proprietary methodologies and innovative IP, I have achieved outstanding results. I've developed a unique leadership model called Ascension Leadership, accompanied by a transformative 12-week program designed to help business owners evolve from entrepreneurs to CEOs with gravitas and a strong sense of self.

My vision extends beyond individual transformation. I aim to introduce this program to corporate environments, particularly male-dominated sectors like mining and engineering, where the principles of empathy and effective leadership are crucial.

As a thought leader in my field, I take immense pride in helping business owners implement systems that enhance team capability, elevate business performance, and accelerate results. I serve as a virtual COO, equipping business owners with the tools and confidence to manage their businesses successfully.

My journey has been one of resilience, determination, and unwavering commitment to personal and professional growth. From overcoming personal tragedy and navigating the complexities of corporate life to reclaiming my identity and financial stability, I've learned that our greatest challenges often reveal our true strengths. Today, my mission is clear: to empower business owners to realise their full potential through effective systems and leadership.

As you reach the end of this chapter, I urge you to reflect on your journey. Sometimes, our dreams' beauty and worth are not immediately visible. We may find ourselves caught in the grind, unable to see the bigger picture. In these moments, having someone to hold the vision for us becomes invaluable. Every business owner I have worked with has shown me the transformative power of support, guidance, and a shared vision.

I believe in your potential to achieve greatness. Whether you are just starting your business or looking to scale new heights, remember that you have the power within you to overcome any obstacle. Surround yourself with those who see your potential and believe in your dreams as much as you do. Let their vision and support guide you when the path seems unclear.

My call to action for you is simple:

Embrace your vision.Seek out the right systems and leadership skills.Connect deeply with your purpose.

Do this, and you will achieve your dreams and have a lasting impact on your business, your community, and beyond.

Together, we can build a future where businesses thrive, leaders inspire, and dreams become reality. I am here to support you every step of the way. Let's embark on this journey of growth and success together.

ANGELA SEDRAN

Strategy Execution and Authentic Leadership
Thought Leader, Professional Speaker
and Bestselling Author

https://esys.io/s/angela-sedran-sbi

Rachel WingMan
Triple Happiness Coach

ABOUT THE AUTHOR: RACHEL WINGMAN

Rachel WingMan, based in Sydney, is a dynamic **Triple Happiness Coach** who combines the best of Asian and Western cultures to focus on glowing skin, a healthy body, and a happy mind. She champions the **3H happy formula—Happiness, Health, and Habits**, supported by her innovative **3-2-1 strategy**—comprising 3-tools (knowledge & skill, people, experience), 2-self-reflection questions, and 1-book each month—to help clients achieve holistic well-being.

As the founder of **Wonderlab and PORES X**, Rachel revolutionises skincare, promoting accessible, affordable, and sustainable beauty.

In this digital age, Rachel believes that anything is possible with the right approach and continued learning. She is committed to empowering individuals, groups, and businesses to reach their full potential by focusing on a balanced life across key areas: Health, Family & Friends, Relationships, Work, Finances, Fun/Adventures, Hobbies, Sleep Quality, Emotions, and Community Activities. Her coaching is deeply rooted in a gratitude mindset and self-reflection, emphasising resilience and the ability to transform challenges into opportunities. Passionate about community building and education, she aims to expand her influence and cultivate a network that values holistic wellness.

Rachel lives by her motto: "Make sure today's ME is better than yesterday, and tomorrow's ME is better than today," inspiring continuous growth and achievement. **Connect with Rachel to explore how she can help you navigate your path to happiness and success.**

CHAPTER 2

GRATITUDE IN MOTION: RACHEL WINGMAN'S JOURNEY FROM ADVERSITY TO EMPOWERMENT

By Rachel WingMan

My Journey to a New Beginning

At 15, I landed alone in my new home in Australia, a country vastly different from my native Hong Kong. Knowing no one and with no grasp of English, my journey was challenging—from battling a disfiguring skin condition to adapting to a new culture. These early hardships were the forge upon which my resilience was tempered and my passion for life was kindled.

"Life is about enjoying, not whinging, regardless of the challenges ahead!" This mantra has guided me through a life that has transitioned from overcoming bullying and cultural shocks to pioneering holistic wellness. Today, as The Triple Happiness Coach, I help people achieve a healthy body, a happy mind through gratitude and glowing, healthy skin.

I was born into a traditional Chinese family in Hong Kong. My parents were loving blue-collar workers with limited education. Their lives revolved around work, leaving little time for anything else. Despite this, they didn't pressure us about education; they focused on work because they knew no life but the grind of hard work, a mentality ingrained by society and generations before them. Their world was survival, where every moment was about earning and saving.

As a child, I was emotionally fragile and unable to handle bullying due to my disfiguring psoriasis. I was often overwhelmed by tears. My worried parents didn't know how to help, so I was forced to cope on my own. The stress severely impacted my self-esteem.

A Turning Point

My turning point came at 14 when I participated in an overseas study tour. It was a breakthrough moment, and I knew I had to change the trajectory of my life. With newfound determination, I convinced my worried parents to let me study abroad. Their hesitant agreement was pivotal in my life, filled with promise and fear.

Encountering New Challenges

Australia came with different challenges. I was bullied due to the language barrier. A misunderstanding led to isolation from potential new friends, and the culture shock was more intense than I'd imagined. Homesickness set in, but I coped by journaling, something I still practise nearly three decades later.

My first return home was joyful yet heartbreakingly brief. Tragically, just days before I was due to return to Australia, my father died in a car accident. Devastated, I matured rapidly as I supported my mother through her grief and funeral arrangements. Yet, even in such a dark time, my mother encouraged me to return to Australia—a testament to her strength and support.

Choosing My Path

After deliberating on how staying or going would impact my future. I chose Australia, a painful but empowering decision. I learned that life doesn't always follow a plan—we must be flexible and open to finding our way through unexpected challenges.

"Self-reflection moment" *Like me, have you ever stood at a crossroads, knowing each path would irrevocably change your life? What did you choose?*

Breaking the Norm

In Hong Kong, society defines a "good kid" as someone who excels academically, achieves financial success and material wealth, and obeys their parents unquestioningly. My encounters with bullying inspired me to chart my course, so I established my criteria by prioritising enjoyment during my school years instead of fixating on grades. I even played truant in going to karaoke and roller skating!

For my university studies, I chose a degree in Multimedia and Arts, a field far removed from the traditional professions valued by my community. I was not driven by societal approval but by a genuine love for creativity and expression.

Entrepreneurial Spirit

Upon graduating, I chose entrepreneurship over employment. Inspired by my part-time jobs in a sandwich shop and an Italian café, I opened King Sandwiches in Hong Kong during the SARS crisis, taking advantage of lower rents. Setting up the business was exhilarating—from designing the logo and menu to learning about coffee and barista skills.

However, the reality of running a business soon set in. Long hours, complex operations, and financial constraints took their toll. When it came time to renew the lease at a much higher rate, I faced the tough decision to close. Returning to Australia, I was grateful for the experience instead of being disheartened.

Lessons Learned and New Beginnings

Running a business requires a deep understanding of everything from accounting to operations. Despite ending, my first business venture was a rich learning experience that set the stage for future successes.

Looking back, I realise how each step and decision shaped the person I am today. By embracing the gratitude mindset, I've transformed challenges into stepping stones, always moving forward with an open heart and a will to succeed.

"Self-reflection moment" *What has failure taught you about resilience? The closing of my sandwich shop was a hard lesson, but it paved the way for more tremendous success. Can you recall a failure that set the stage for a later triumph in your life?*

Reinvention: A Journey Through Design and Marketing

Back in Australia, I was lucky to land a job as a graphic designer at an IT hardware company. I was excited to apply what I had learned in school to create incredible designs. However, I quickly realised that the company's idea of the best design was based on the owners' subjective tastes rather than user experience or consumer feedback. This was disheartening, as I felt I was just following orders rather than being a creative contributor.

After 18 months, I decided to switch from graphic design to marketing. This change allowed me to oversee projects more comprehensively, focusing on aesthetics and the strategic outcomes that drove business success. I took a marketing course to prepare for my new role, enhancing my design skills with foundational marketing principles.

This role was a turning point, teaching me the importance of prioritising results over details. I am thankful for this position's clarity, enabling me to adapt and advance my career from design to marketing quickly. This transition led to a flexible marketing role in IT, which allowed me to work from home three days a week and balance my responsibilities as a mother while still being productive in my career.

Embarking on a Path to Wellness and Community Building

I started The Mummy Club Blog and quickly gained 7,000 followers. Unfortunately, the business closed after a partnership dispute. However, I pivoted and established the Family Fun Planner community, where I shared family-friendly travel itineraries, quickly gaining another 5,000 followers.

I still struggled with ongoing skin conditions—eczema and breakouts—that no one was able to solve. This ongoing battle with my skin laid the groundwork for a significant shift in my career trajectory.

In 2017, my sister needed support after divorcing her husband due to a gambling addiction. Without hesitation, I invited her and her young daughter to Australia. At the time, I supported my youngest sister with her studies in Australia. Fortunately, my husband and I had the financial stability to support my extended family and ourselves.

Seeing an opportunity to provide for my sister and leverage her extensive experience in the beauty industry, I opened a small salon called Wonderlab. I saw the potential to build something more significant instead of just a job for her. Thanks to her expertise and dedication, Wonderlab quickly established a strong client base in a highly competitive market.

Wonderlab and Beyond: Learning, Growing, and Innovating

The success at Wonderlab and the improvements in my skin health—achieved not through expensive treatments but through simple, consistent care—convinced me of the beauty industry's potential.

However, just a week after the grand opening of our expanded Wonderlab facilities, the world plunged into the chaos of the first COVID-19 lockdown. Faced with this unprecedented challenge, I focused on proactive strategies to keep my team engaged and our business afloat. Leveraging government subsidies, I encouraged our staff to enhance their digital skills, spending 8 to 10 hours a week developing new social media skills. This helped maintain our connection with clients through regular updates and engagement on platforms like Facebook and prepared our team for a more digital future in beauty and wellness.

The lockdowns taught us resilience and adaptability. After the initial shock, Wonderlab returned to a semblance of normalcy with busy bookings, only to be hit by a second wave of COVID. This challenge pushed me to reassess my career in the context of a global company. The disconnect and relentless Zoom meetings across time zones sapped my work of joy, prompting a decisive career shift—I left to invest fully in my passion for wellness.

"Self-reflection moment" *When faced with a crisis that disrupts everything, how do you respond?*

The Power of a Simple Act of Kindness

I believe in the "giver's gain" philosophy, which promotes the mutual benefits of giving. This belief guided me in creating Wonderlab, which not only helped my sister but also laid the foundation for a larger wellness empire. This experience taught me that the path to creating an empire can sometimes begin with a simple act of kindness. The wellness empire I now lead was born from the desire to help a distressed family member and has grown into a beacon of community and support.

The Genesis of PORES X: Revolutionising Skincare

PORES X was created to make skincare simple, inclusive, and adaptable to every lifestyle. My transition from IT to beauty revealed a gap in the market. Quality skincare was often considered a luxury rather than a necessity, only accessible to those who could afford the time and expense. PORES X aims to empower everyone to achieve their best skin by combining technology, education, and habit-forming techniques, making high-quality skincare accessible to all, regardless of time, age, gender, or financial situation.

With simple, fixed-price services and no hidden costs, PORES X eliminated the traditional barriers to skincare. We use the latest technology, provide education, and employ habit-forming techniques to encourage consistent skincare routines among our clients. Our mission is to empower individuals to take control of their skin's health without feeling overwhelmed by cost, complexity, or time commitments.

A New Era of Inclusive Beauty

One day, a girlfriend of mine showed me a photo from a college campus. In it, one girl stood out for her natural beauty while her peers resorted to injectables and surgeries in pursuit of perfection. This stark image underscored the urgent need for skincare education—an alternative to the invasive procedures that have become increasingly normal for young adults.

At PORES X, we are dedicated to redefining beauty standards by emphasising education about skin health as much as the treatments we provide. We aim to be a supportive resource for parents guiding their children through skincare routines, especially during the challenging puberty stage.

PORES X aims to break down barriers and create a welcoming, supportive community where beauty is genuinely for everyone.

Challenges and Growth

The journey to establish PORES X was filled with hurdles as we sought to challenge and transform entrenched norms within the beauty industry. To truly innovate, we had to scale our operations quickly, reaching out to a broad demographic often overlooked by traditional skincare providers—those deterred by the high costs and time commitments usually associated with quality skincare.

Our efforts to make skincare accessible and straightforward have resonated deeply, leading to a community of over 300 members in just 20 months. This rapid growth is a business achievement and a validation of our vision. My team, fully aligned with our ethos, has been pivotal in this success. They ensure the smooth running of our daily operations, which frees me up to strategise and foster further growth.

Investing in Vision: A Testament to Commitment and Loving Relationship

My dedication to PORES X transcended typical business risks—I invested directly from our family mortgage, making a significant financial commitment to the business and the community we serve. This monumental step reflected my resolve to see PORES X succeed and my belief in its potential to make a meaningful impact. This investment was also a profound testament to the trust and love between my husband and me. Initially, we both held stable, well-paying corporate jobs, and we came from backgrounds that prized financial security. My husband, in particular, is not one for taking risks. His nature is to avoid the unpredictable, making his support for my entrepreneurial journey all the more significant.

Despite his initial reservations about running our own business, he has stood by my side, motivated by the passion and commitment he sees in me. His support is a gesture of belief in the business's success and an expression of unconditional love. He has ventured outside his comfort zone, embracing a path he once resisted, involving a considerable personal evolution. I am deeply grateful for his backing—it has strengthened our relationship and reinforced my determination to make PORES X a beacon of innovative skincare solutions.

This journey has not just been about building a business but about nurturing a partnership where personal and professional growth are interlinked.

"Self-reflection moment" *Have you ever faced a decision that scared you, yet you knew it was right? Choosing to invest our family's savings into starting PORES X was terrifying, but my conviction was clear. What fears have you faced head-on for the sake of something more significant?*

Cultivating the GlowTogether and GrowTogether Culture

At the heart of all my businesses lies the foundational mantra: "GlowTogether, GrowTogether." This philosophy encapsulates our commitment to fostering a supportive and inclusive environment where each individual is encouraged to shine and contribute to the collective growth of our community.

"Self-reflection moment" *Looking back, the trials of those early days taught me more than resilience—they sculpted my understanding of gratitude. I learned to find a silver lining in every challenge, which became my guiding light. What lessons have your challenges taught you?*

Turning Challenges into More Opportunity: The Birth of Rachel Wing Man Happiness Coaching

Navigating the upheaval of COVID-19 made me realise that something fundamental had shifted. Across our three retail outlets, it became clear that our clients were seeking more than just skincare or relaxation treatments; they were looking for human connection and a release from the mounting pressures of a rapidly changing world. The pandemic had escalated anxiety and stress levels, making the financial strains and social isolation almost unbearable for many.

This profound insight led me to delve deeper into positive psychology and Neuro-Linguistic Programming (NLP). My goal was to understand the intricacies of the human mind and apply this knowledge to help others find more happiness.

As someone with an IT background, I have witnessed the AI revolution firsthand. While many people fear and distrust it, I view AI as a tool that can improve our quality of life by freeing up our time and enabling us to focus on what truly matters—our well-being. It was time to shift the focus from merely surviving in this high-tech age to thriving, leading me to recognise an urgent need for strategies prioritising mental health and overall well-being.

The Genesis of a New Coaching Philosophy

So, Rachel Wing Man Happiness Coaching was born, a synthesis of my learning and experiences tailored to empower individuals. My Chinese name, 'Wing Man,' meaning protecting and helping others, seemed predestined for this role. My coaching method utilises the 3-2-1 strategies, focused on three foundational pillars: Mindset, Energy, and Relationships. This structured approach includes employing three practical tools for daily life, engaging in two self-reflection questions to foster deeper learning, and committing to reading one transformative book each week. Together, these elements create a dynamic environment where clients can grow, learn, and achieve holistic happiness for themselves and their children.

It's crucial not to adhere to tradition or accept societal standards for us and our children. Our beliefs and how we raise our children significantly impact their happiness and resilience. Clinging to outdated methods can stifle their potential and hinder growth from embracing new perspectives.

Change is not just inevitable; it is essential for growth. We must reflect on our behaviours and beliefs as we strive to raise a healthier, happier next generation. Are we perpetuating cycles that limit our children's potential and happiness? This question requires honesty and can lead to profound shifts in how we support our children's development.

Cultivating New Mindsets

The power of a diverse mindset cannot be underestimated, yet it's not something that can be switched on like a light. It requires consistent practice and commitment. Many of us fall into the trap of trying a new approach once and abandoning it while still waiting for immediate results. However, developing the right behaviours and emotional responses is more like training a muscle—it strengthens with regular use.

I see myself as a personal trainer for the mind and heart. Like a physical trainer adjusts exercise routines to help you reach your fitness goals, I guide clients through mental and emotional workouts. These exercises are designed to cultivate resilience and gratitude, emphasising a broader range of skills beyond academic accomplishments, which are insufficient for thriving in today's world.

Building Resilience and Gratitude in the Next Generation

Resilience is critical for our children. It's about bouncing "forward" from setbacks and forging ahead with confidence and adaptability. By cultivating gratitude and resilience, not just academic success, we empower them to face life's challenges head-on.

As a happiness coach, my role goes beyond simple guidance. I am here to motivate, support, and empower you and your family on your journey to a fulfilling life. It's about creating strategies to proactively address challenges rather than reacting impulsively, fostering a healthier, more balanced approach to everyday stresses.

As we shape the next generation, let's reflect on our development. Are we reactive or proactive? It's time to embody the changes we want to see in our children and create paths for holistic growth and happiness.

Looking Forward

The experiences I've faced have shown me the significance of gratitude. It has been the catalyst for my personal transformation and forms the foundation of the Rachel Wing Man Happiness Coaching philosophy. Our mission is to assist people in navigating the complexities of modern life, helping them survive and thrive.

"Self-reflection moment" *What are you grateful for today? How can expressing gratitude change your perspective on difficult situations?*

Community forms the heart of all my businesses. The mantra "Glow Together, Grow Together" encapsulates our commitment to building a supportive community where everyone is encouraged to shine. This ethos is woven into Wonderlab, PORES X, and Rachel Wing Man, creating a space where people can come together to share, learn, and support each other in their journeys to happiness.

I'm not striving to become a legend. I believe in the transformative power of individual influence. I understand that positively impacting even a single person or assisting a parent in creating a happier family can make a difference.

My achievements are not measured by awards but by spreading happiness. This goal drives everything I do. By promoting small, positive changes, I aim to create a community where collective happiness grows, showing that significant impacts can stem from nurturing joy and resilience in every person.

Join Our Happiness Community

As you reach the final page of this chapter, our conversation doesn't have to end here. I invite you to share your thoughts, challenges, and insights with me.

Do you have questions about navigating life's challenges, or do you wish to share how you've applied gratitude and resilience? Perhaps you're seeking advice on how to encourage well-being in your family or community. Whatever your query or story, I am here to listen.

Let's inspire and support each other, creating a community where we grow and shine together. Together, we can actively shape and improve our lives, turning challenges into opportunities for growth and happiness. I look forward to hearing from you and exploring how we can live more fulfilling lives through mutual support and shared wisdom.

Connect with Rachel WingMan.

Please reach out to me at https://rachelwm.com.au/.

YouTube: https://www.youtube.com/@RachelWingman

Instagram: https://www.instagram.com/rachelwingman.co/

Facebook: https://www.facebook.com/profile.php?id=61557378170783

Tik Tok: https://www.tiktok.com/@rachelwingman?lang=en

Key Takeaways

- **Embrace Change:** Embrace change for personal growth. Adapting to new roles, such as parenthood, leadership, or community involvement, requires a shift in mindset to support the next generation effectively.

- **Cultivate Resilience**: Developing a resilient, positive mindset is a lifelong practice that enhances our ability to navigate life's challenges.

- **Nurture Holistic Wellbeing**: True success encompasses more than just physical health; it includes emotional and mental wellbeing, essential for a fulfilling life.

- **Build Community**: We empower each other to overcome obstacles and achieve our dreams by fostering a supportive environment.

- **Practise Gratitude:** Gratitude transforms challenges into opportunities, teaching us to value each experience and find joy and lessons in every situation.
- **Self-Reflect**: Self-reflection is a powerful tool for personal development. It encourages us to look inward and examine our thoughts, beliefs, and actions.

RACHEL WINGMAN

Triple Happiness Coach

https://esys.io/s/rachel-wm

Jenny Godfrey
Mum, Digital Marketing Strategist and Author

ABOUT THE AUTHOR: JENNY GODFREY

Over twenty years ago, Jenny Godfrey realised the world of marketing was on the cusp of significant digital media growth. This was the perfect opportunity for her to start her own digital marketing business – even though she was a young mum in a new city.

In 2024, Jenny's company, Concept Designs & Marketing, has grown to include a team of marketing consultants, experts, designers, website developers, Google and Meta ads specialists, SEO experts and content writers. All members continue to remain on the cutting edge of the latest marketing strategies.

Looking back, Jenny feels validated by her 2001 decision to remain in the industry and keep her finger on the pulse. It has meant she can offer her clients over two decades of up-to-date experience across a variety of industries when it comes to determining marketing strategies that are best suited for individual businesses and industries.

As a marketing strategist, Jenny's highest priority is to listen to the needs and goals of your business and brand, then work with you to determine the target market and the best strategies to reach them.

When it comes to website design and development, lead generation through Google or Meta ads, website conversions, or LinkedIn optimisation, Jenny and her team ensure your website and your business are found quickly by your target market.

If you're feeling the fast-paced change in the marketing industry, you're not alone. In fact, with the introduction of AI into the marketing scene, Jenny predicts these constant changes are only going to continue.

Jenny is committed to remaining at the forefront of marketing and design innovation. Her focus lies in creating marketing strategies that align with the business goals of her clients, and ensuring they receive the best return on investment for their marketing dollars.

CHAPTER 3

RAISING A (FAMILY) BUSINESS

By Jenny Godfrey

When our twin boys were eighteen months old, I started my business totally unaware I would soon be expecting our third child. Now, as I write this chapter, one of my adult children is planning their wedding.

I'm writing this for all the mums who wonder how they can raise a family and a business at the same time.

Impossible, right?

No.

I'm here to say it can be done but it's not a journey for the fainthearted. It's hard but it's also fun.

I've often wondered what I would say to my younger self. What lessons have I learned, and applied, that would be worth sharing?

Then I thought, 'Why not write about it?'

The Meeting: Younger Me Meets Older Me

The Young Entrepreneur

Like most days, I'd woken early and tired. I slurped down some tea and ate a slice of toast, scribbling notes and filling my to-do list. After a walk around the block with our Border Collie, Cody, I was ready for my first meeting of the day.

My little side business had been slowly gaining momentum. I had energy and focus. There were always books to read, and courses to take, but I needed more. I needed guidance. Magically, at just the right time, I'd received a mysterious invitation to meet with a seasoned professional.

I walked through the cafe doors and scanned the room.

The Seasoned Professional

I woke early to my familiar alarm, 'I've got you babe'. Enough time to squeeze in some exercise and a little meditation, while thinking about the day ahead.

I often visited Spencer's Cafe when I was much younger, purchasing babychinos and pulling out pencils and paper to keep my children amused while I worked. And here I was again; ready to meet with a long-time friend.

I'd had time to think about the experiences and memories I wanted to share and relive.

Then suddenly, here she was; right on time – evidence of her trademark tenacity and discipline. Her hair was cut just above her shoulders, the 'mum' cut so in vogue at the time. Professional and efficient. Despite the hint of puffiness around her eyes, her face was full of optimism and energy.

The Young Entrepreneur

The moment I saw her, there was a deep sense of familiarity; however, I was confused. Was this even possible?

I sighed. The years were starting to show, but she seemed more self-assured with the usual trappings of success – jewellery, fine clothes, brand accessories. She wore bold colours with confidence and addressed the staff by their names.

Tentatively, I approached the older me. How should I introduce myself? Did I even need to?

Smiling, she motioned me to sit. An open notebook revealed the start of a new list: *Things I've learned today*. Humility – a realisation she hadn't yet arrived at – coupled with experience, understanding and knowledge.

Do we ever really 'arrive'?

I edged forward, ready to listen to her stories and be reminded that what lay ahead would be both hard and fun. More than anything, I was ready to learn how she grew her business without compromising her first priority – family.

Here's what she told me.

- **Work-life balance within flexible working hours**

Stepping back into a career after starting a family is hard, but around 40% of women do this. You're not alone.

Things transition quickly. Once, it was the advent of websites and the internet; now, it's tech advances and social media. It never slows down. Keep your finger on the pulse. Keep up with the trends and changes so your clients don't have to.

As your business expands, juggling work, family and personal time becomes harder. You have to find balance. Paying attention to indicators of overwhelm and understanding why you're feeling this way are essential.

Pew Research Centre[1] suggests 74% of working mothers feel guilty about not being present enough for their children. For me, it was work commitments impacting family time, but I was determined to overcome this.

I remember the February 2011 swimming carnival. Our children were in Years 5 and 3 and had been at their new school for less than three weeks. I didn't want to miss their first carnival with their new friends, so with camping chair and computer, I made the pool my office for the day.

It worked. I volunteered for set-up and familiarised myself with the schedule so I was poolside to cheer my children on as they raced. I bought them snow cones and saw them receive their participation ribbons. And, I got work done.

That day, I modelled the value of quality time and work-life balance. I got it right. Flexible work hours allowed me to achieve a work-life balance where family and business both had their place at the right time. I didn't always get it right but I knew it was achievable and it reduced my overall stress.

It's not only me. According to Gallup[2], 60% of women consider work-life balance very important.

- **Enhance your skills, discover your strengths, understand your core values**

At some point in your life, you'll discover a desire to understand who you are – your personality, your strengths and why you do what you do. Knowing this made me a more rounded mum and CEO who operated from a deep commitment to what I valued. Your core values filter their way into your business – your team, client selection, interactions and how you respond to different situations.

I did my first psychometric test when my husband Dave and I were at college. It taught us about our personalities, and how we perceived the world and made decisions. At the time, what struck me most was how different Dave and I were – the complete opposite. As a young, relatively newlywed couple, this was an eye-opener and helped me understand how we worked best together.

My next psychometric test measured my innate talents and showed me how to turn them into strengths. This test was introduced along the lines of 'Why do we alwayss push ourselves with more education and more learning to improve an area we know we lack in?' In other words, why try to improve weaknesses, when we could develop strengths?

Maybe I misinterpreted the aim of this psychometric test, but I resonated with that approach.

This test told me what my top five strengths were out of a list of forty. I was told they only give the top five because otherwise, everyone goes to the end to see their weakest qualities.

Psychometric testing is a big part of our family. Dave uses it as a tool at his places of work. We've taken our family and team members through the test because the results help us know one another, and release us to do what we do best.

As life changed and I moved into a new phase, I became invested in other psychometric testing with my business coaches. These included DiSC, Extended DiSC, and Core Values. These, alongside Myers-Briggs and Gallup StrengthFinder, have been powerful formation tools for me as a leader in my business.

I've found so much value in discovering who I am as a person and leader. As the team at Concept Designs & Marketing grows, we use it to help the team discover their strengths and abilities – and where their genius is – so we can structure opportunities for maximum team engagement and allow each team member to find their unique place.

Why is this so important?

For us, it has brought incredible cohesion and unity to our team and has allowed me to empower team members.

When it's your turn to go through it, enjoy it. Recognise it's a stage of life and use it to help understand how you respond in certain situations.

- **Build, invest and collaborate within your business networks**

Whenever I felt isolated in my endeavours as a woman in business or felt like I lacked robust professional or personal support networks, I intentionally leaned into the strong business networks I've developed over the years. Nurturing those relationships has been valuable because they have led to new opportunities and amazing support systems.

I didn't realise this until 2011 when I joined two business networks on the Gold Coast (The Business League and BNI). Both networks have introduced me to incredible business owners over the years and reduced feelings of isolation as a woman in business. You meet some amazing people in networking; my business relationships have become some of my best friends.

I've been networking for years. Just this year, I was attending the BNI Sydney North East awards breakfast as a member sponsor. Out of nearly 300 members, I received the award for regional member of the year. I was incredibly humbled and shocked. Hearing my name announced still blows me away. Building strong business networks is key to developing effective word-of-mouth marketing.

As marketers, I believe we can't overlook the power of word-of-mouth marketing; it's something I speak with our clients about. It's the most effective form of marketing, but nowadays business owners have to couple it with other marketing strategies to get cut-through within very busy marketplaces. What I love about my business networking groups is that they are an opportunity for me to take the first couple of hours each week to work on the word-of-mouth marketing strategy for our business – a strategy that's helped me grow our business significantly.

The Seasoned Professional

As I sat across the table, lamenting that our time together was soon coming to a close, I sat in silence for what felt like minutes, but was precisely three seconds. In those moments, it occurred to me that I had also learned valuable life lessons from my younger self in the time we had together. I'd come to this meeting with the intention of 'telling the younger Jenny what I have learned after over twenty years in business', but what I hadn't realised until just now was that I would be leaving our conversation with a reminder of the energy and vigour required to start a new business. Somewhere within me I'd tapped into the past and remembered the discipline and tenacity required of a mum of young children who is starting a business.

The Young Entrepreneur
I didn't want this time to come to an end. There was so much to learn. I was ill-equipped but wanted to strive to make this work. I was overwhelmed but renewed. I was scared and I was emboldened.

What happens when all these emotions collide?

I felt it was making way for a clearly defined path that bends, twists, turns and presents unexpected outcomes from time to time. There was so much more The Seasoned Professional could've told me, The Young Entrepreneur. In the end, she just passed me a napkin with this written diagram:

The Framework

Three disciplines for raising a business

BALANCE

business, relationships, family

INVEST	**ENHANCE**
contribute, collaborate, build	skills, strengths, core values

It was a wet Saturday morning – a typical winter morning with young children who loved soccer. We were driving out to Kenthurst where the fog settled and made for very cold mornings on the sideline.

We'd left home in a rush to make it to the game on time, and I hadn't been able to find my usual chair to sit on the sidelines, so I grabbed the first chair my hands brushed past. It wasn't until we arrived at the game I realised which chair I'd grabbed. It was our old three-legged stool. How on earth was I going to sit on this chair? How was I going to stay upright the whole game with sodden winter ground underfoot? I had no confidence this old three-legged stool was going to do the job, but it did.

Then it hit me – life is like this moment.

Life gets busy. We get flustered. It feels like the soggy ground underfoot is conspiring to leave us in an embarrassed heap, wallowing in the mud. We doubt whether that old three-legged stool will keep us upright.

It did that day, and it does in life – so long as we take care of each of the three legs.

The stability of the stool came from three legs working together. Trying to stay upright on one or two legs takes a lot of energy and almost always ends in disaster.

Enough of the metaphor, now to practicalities.

BALANCE

Balancing family, relationships and business

How do we find balance as parents and in all the significant relationships that fill our lives?

Being a parent doesn't mean giving our children all they want, all the time. It is, however, about striking that balance. There will always be non-negotiables, whether attending a swimming carnival, sitting through a dance concert, or being a support during a stressful piano recital.

Conversely, our children also need enough independence to experience, explore and find satisfaction in the rhythms of life without mum and dad hovering all the time. It can cause an imbalance by giving them everything.

Just as being a parent is full of responsibility, so is running a business. I am unable to give every client everything they want. However, if I know my core values, I can help clients understand what I can do for them, what I can do well and what I can't do.

I am often reminded of Stephen Covey's four quadrants in his book, *The 7 Habits of Highly Effective People*[3]:

1. The urgent and important
2. The urgent and not important
3. The non-urgent and important
4. The non-urgent and not important

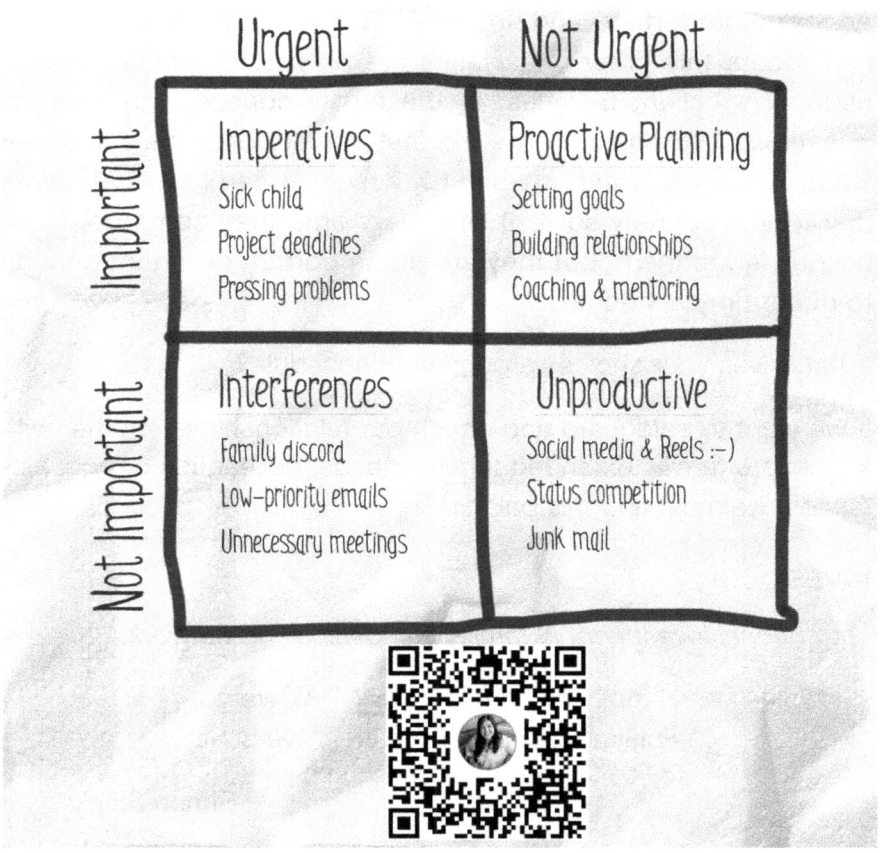

Some things are simply non-urgent and not important. They're the easy ones.

In a sense, the urgent and important tasks that need attention immediately are also easy. For me, it might be a sick child or a client's website that has gone down – they can not and should not be ignored.

Important and not urgent is about being proactive. It's about being able to determine whether I have to do this now, or whether it can be rescheduled to another time.

As for not important, and urgent – in business, there is very little that meets this criteria, as tasks are only as urgent as a team member or client believes. In the family context, this may be questions, such as who ate the last cookie, or decisions about what movie we watch on Saturday night. I can't stop my work day to immediately solve these every time they come up. I can acknowledge them, but they are not important or urgent enough to dictate my schedule.

What drives your choices around your schedule?

If we want to safeguard and enrich our relationships, whether with immediate family, extended family, friends, colleagues or acquaintances, we must find this balance.

INVEST

- *Intentional investment in family, friendships and networks*

> Happiness comes from WHAT we do.
> Fulfilment comes from WHY we do it.
>
> ~ Simon Sinek[4]

'Investing' is not throwing away your time, money or energy, it is an intentional action and commitment that produces a return.

We all start businesses for different reasons, whether that be freedom, flexibility with your time, control over your job description, security or satisfaction from building a successful business. Whatever the reason – you and your business matter, and that is why I do what I do.

Often behind businesses are families who significantly invest their time, energy and resources. It is super important to genuinely invest in people and their businesses; it isn't all just about making money.

In corporations today, there is a priority on the triple bottom line, which is the concept of balancing fiscal responsibility with environmental and social responsibilities. One of the bottom lines of Concept Designs & Marketing is to empower our clients to succeed – facilitating their businesses to succeed. We do that by investing in them, not just their business.

On a practical level, in business there may be someone who is cheaper or who runs a different business model; perhaps someone more charismatic or influential than you. Changes to the market or other external factors that you cannot control may also occur. However, I have found that simply being yourself and sincerely investing in people and their businesses can build extraordinary loyalty from clients and customers.

360 Degree Investment

Invest up

Pay for a business coach or mentor. Take someone who has more experience than you or who understands an aspect of business better than you out for lunch. Learn from them.

Invest horizontally

Network with other business leaders. What they are learning can be of use. Your next lead might, and often does, come from their networks.

Investing horizontally can also include clients. Business is not just about making money, it is about empowering others and helping them succeed. Getting to know my clients – their birthdays or significant moments – means I am more likely to be able to help them personally when an opportunity comes my way.

Horizontal investing also includes investing in the most important people in my life – my family. We have a saying: 'Work hard and holiday well'. One of the Godfrey family values is to spend time together, create experiences and holiday well. Intentionally block out family time when work can not creep in and invest in the relationships in your family.

Invest down

Upskill your staff. Empower them to succeed by helping them discover their strengths and work within their area of genius. Their wins are truly my wins.

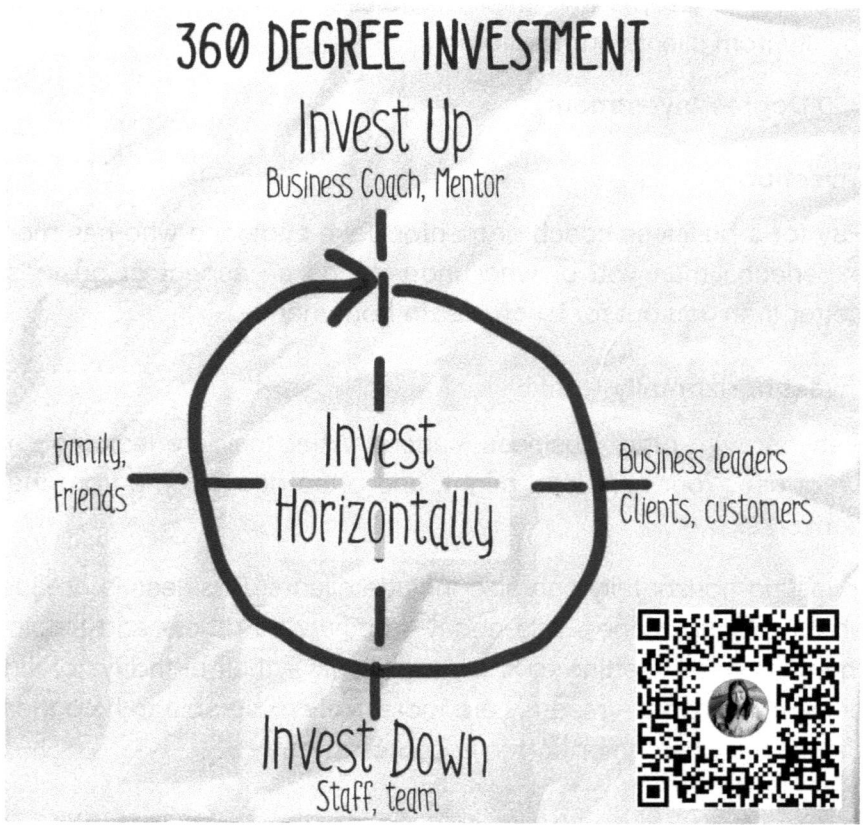

ENHANCE

- Discover, embrace skills and live by your values

The 1989 New York Marathon winner, Juma Ikangaa, said "The will to win means nothing without the will to prepare." Succeeding as a business owner requires dedication, grit and determination. When raising a business – and in many areas of our lives – it takes hard work to achieve our desired outcomes. Part of that work is the preparation to know yourself and your limitations and strengthen yourself. It's akin to a marathon runner preparing for a race.

Experience in business is a commodity only if we are growing and learning. Time alone does not equal experience in business. It is how we choose to use it. If you have been in business for ten years, yet never grow, learn or upskill, then you are a ten-year intern or a start-up entrepreneur who keeps repeating the first year.

Invariably, technologies are changing, and innovation is shaping our experiences. If we don't grow and develop skills, then we risk becoming as obsolete as our flip phones and DVD players. This involves upskilling, whether that be through courses, reading, podcasts or conferences, and engagement with mentors.

Often, when people start their business they do all things for all people and have to be an all-rounder. Over time, they grow and transition into working within their sphere of strength and hiring to supplement areas where gaps appear. This paves the way for growing a sustainable business that leaves a legacy.

Many psychometric tools are available to tease out our strengths, measure our skills and uncover our personality traits. While you don't want to use these tests to 'box yourself in', nor to 'be boxed in', they can be helpful to dig deeper and help you understand things about yourself that you were previously unaware of. They can also provide external affirmation of things you instinctively felt were your strengths.

On the other hand, our core values are our innate, individual non-negotiables. They are our authentic guiding principles that we will not lay down. They ensure our actions consistently align with our personal beliefs. And one will often find they are more motivated and more fulfilled in their areas of work when their convictions and core values align within their job.

I would like to leave you with one encouragement – one final challenge – dig in and discover your core values.

In *Dare to Lead*, Brene Brown shares a list of values and challenges us to actively engage our values. She says:

Living into our values means that we do more than profess our values, we practice them. We walk our talk – we are clear about what we believe, and hold important, and we take care that our intentions, words, thoughts and behaviours align with those beliefs.[5]

My passion for raising both a great family and a great business is reflected in my clientele, many of whom are also balancing family and work commitments.

Why is this? I simply have a strong affinity with families because I understand what it takes to raise a successful business with a young family. I understand the sacrifices and the hours that this requires. I understand the juggle between finishing a client meeting at the kitchen bench, and then turning around to start cooking dinner.

If you'd like more information about the framework or how I made this work for me, visit my website: jennygodfrey.au, or scan the QR codes in the chapter.

JENNY GODFREY

Mum, Digital Marketing Strategist and Author

https://esys.io/s/jenny-godfrey

1. Pew Research Center. (2012). Women, work, and motherhood. In The Harried Life of the Working Mother. Pew Research Center. Retrieved from https://www.pewresearch.org

2. Gallup. (2023). Employee Engagement. In Understanding Work-Life Balance. Retrieved from Gallup

3. Covey, S. R. (1989). The 7 Habits of Highly Effective People: Powerful Lessons in Personal Change. Free Press. (Chapter 3)

4. Sinek, S. (2017). Find Your Why: A Practical Guide for Discovering Purpose for You and Your Team. Penguin Books.

5. Brown, B. (2018). Dare to Lead: Brave Work. Tough Conversations. Whole Hearts. Random House. (p. 186).

Michelle Huntington
Inspirational Keynote Speaker, Leadership Coach,
Podcast Host, Corporate Trainer, and Media Commentator

ABOUT THE AUTHOR: MICHELLE HUNTINGTON

Michelle Huntington's journey, filled with adventure, tenacity, and resilience, propelled her through challenges to achieve her dream of becoming an Airline Captain. In her captivating keynote speeches and forthcoming book, "Keep Going Until You Can't," Michelle shares her daring exploits, illustrating her remarkable courage and innovative spirit in overcoming obstacles.

As an Inspirational Keynote Speaker, Leadership Coach, Corporate Trainer, and media commentator, Michelle draws from over two decades of aviation experience, where she honed her problem-solving skills in high-stakes situations.

Michelle's narratives resonate deeply with audiences, offering practical insights gleaned from her experiences, whether it's making critical decisions with lives at stake or devising ingenious solutions to complex challenges. Her ability to blend storytelling with impactful lessons makes learning both engaging and actionable.

Michelle's adventurous spirit knows no bounds, as evidenced by her diverse array of experiences, ranging from aviation exploration to advocating for Indigenous artists. With aviation coursing through her veins, she has amassed a treasure trove of tales, each a testament to resilience and the pursuit of dreams.

In her upcoming book, Michelle invites readers on a thrilling journey beyond the clouds, sharing anecdotes from the cockpit that are equal parts humorous and heart-stopping, yet always brimming with wisdom and inspiration.

Join Michelle as she demonstrates the power of saying "yes" to life's opportunities and embracing the adventure of the journey. Her book, slated for release in 2024, promises to be a compelling testament to perseverance, laughter, and the fulfillment found in chasing one's dreams.

Why not book Michelle for your next conference?

CHAPTER 4

FLYING SOLO ACROSS THE PACIFIC

By Michelle Huntington

As the aircraft descended through the dense cloud cover, the roar of the engines mingled with palpable tension in the cockpit. While turbulence rattled the cabin, the captain's unexpected words cut through the air like a sharp gust of wind, echoing a doubt that threatened to overshadow my dreams, "You know Michelle, I don't think you'll be a good Captain."

"Pardon?" I responded, taken aback.

I was navigating a precarious instrument approach into Hamilton Island, and his comment was wholly inappropriate for the situation. The short airstrip was notorious for its challenges, especially in gusty, poor weather like this.

Setting aside my frustration with his incredibly poor timing, I focused on executing a flawless textbook landing, ensuring a gentle kiss on the runway within the designated touchdown zone. This sector marked my final flight as a First Officer. Nine years with the airline had led to this moment—Command School, the path to becoming a Captain.

Once the passengers disembarked and preparations for the return flight were complete, I couldn't hold back any longer.

"Why did you say that to me on approach?"

"Don't take it personally," he replied. "It's not just you. I don't think any women make good Captains."

He was right: Women don't make good Captains; we make great Captains.

As his words echoed through my mind, a resolve ignited in me. I had overcome far greater challenges than being subjected to stupid and senseless remarks to get here. His scepticism and misogyny paled against my conviction to achieve my dream.

During my school years overseas, colouring competitions were common entertainment for the children of RAAF employees. The prizes were exhilarating joy flights aboard various military aircraft. The prizes and safety standards, reflecting on it now, seem almost absurd. It was winning one of these colouring-in competitions when I was 5 years old that ignited my dream of becoming a pilot.

I won a flight aboard a Mirage Fighter jet trainer—a surreal opportunity for a mere five-year-old, barely tall enough to see out the front window. Imagine being strapped securely into the cockpit with a five-point harness, and receiving a stern safety briefing of, "Don't touch anything!" I was giddy with a blend of excitement and trepidation for the adventure.

The scent of burnt kerosene filled the air as I was thrust back into my seat. Feeling every G-force as the aircraft climbed vertically. Like a roller-coaster ride, I experienced weightlessness for what felt like an eternity, but really lasted only seconds. I screamed all the way back down.

I wasn't screaming with fright; It was pure excitement. It was exhilarating.

I couldn't wipe the smile off my face when we landed.

I was captivated!

Having viewed the world from above, a dream was ignited.

"I can do that," I thought to myself. "I need to be a pilot."

A decade later, that dream would be challenged.

"What do you want to be when you grow up, Michelle?" asked my school career advisor, a rehearsed line betraying her lack of genuine interest.

"A Pilot," I replied, anticipating her encouragement.

"Ha! Michelle, women can't be pilots!" she scoffed.

"Why not?" I asked, surprised by her dismissive attitude.

"Oh Michelle, women are different from men," she asserted.

Obviously, I thought to myself.

"For women to be pilots, they'd have to wear a tampon every time they flew so their guts wouldn't fall out," she added, her words dripping with ignorance, prejudice and more than a touch of stupidity.

It was absurd, backward, and utterly disheartening that in the late 1980s, a 'guide' for the next generation held such antiquated views.

In the end, feeling the weight of societal expectations, I obediently followed the path she suggested, enrolling in university to study art. My dream shattered, relegated to the realm of impossibility.

At Uni, I met and married a boy from Gunnedah, who was studying Agriculture. B&S Balls, utes and driving tractors was fun—for a while. The isolation of endless days on a cotton farm began to gnaw at me, turning monotony into a suffocating solitude.

I craved more than farm life could offer.

Time passed, my husband and I drifted apart, leaving me to navigate the waters of motherhood with a young son in tow. A change of scenery beckoned. With my little boy, I set my sights on a fresh start.

It was in Tamworth, amidst the hustle and bustle of semi-urban life, where I said perhaps the most absurd comment of my life. Having endured the loneliness of farm life, I had sought out new connections, joining a mixed Oz tag team to expand my social circle.

On the first night of training, I met the only other woman on the team. Engaging in small talk, I learned she was a student pilot at the British Aerospace Flight Training Academy. I was astonished—a woman, defying gender prejudice to pursue her passion for flight? Before I could stop myself, I blurted out, "But what about the tampons?" My words stumbling over each other, and I couldn't seem to stop. "Do you use them on every flight? To stop your guts from spilling out?"

I still cringe at this memory, yet in that moment, amidst laughter and her disbelief, my dormant dream of taking to the skies was reignited, fuelled by the determination of a fellow woman defying convention.

My dream to be a pilot was back on!

Learning to fly is expensive, so I approached the bank for a loan. They refused to finance a woman's aspiration to take to the skies. Undeterred by this familiar theme, I refused to let it derail my dreams.

I went to another bank, spun a tale about home renovations and secured the loan I needed.

With funds in hand, I embarked on a drastic course of action. I liquidated all my assets, selling my house and car to finance my dream. Moving back in with my mother and young son, I committed every cent to prepaid flying lessons, determined to become a pilot.

My first lesson, that scorching February, thrust me into a whirlwind of nerves. The flying sequences took their toll, and coupled with the sweltering heat, I found myself teetering on the brink of vomiting.

Mouth-watering. Shallow breathing. Drenched in sweat.

I confided in my instructor. I was met with reassurance and a makeshift solution: deep breaths and a cracked storm window for fresh air. Alas, it proved futile. The nausea persisted, but more concerning was the absence of a sick bag. It was inevitable. I was going to be sick.

My instructor directed me to loosen my tie, undo my shirt buttons, and vomit down my top.

Embarrassed but determined, I followed his instructions and let loose inside my shirt. He reached over and adjusted my mouthpiece to spare himself the stereo symphony of retching in his headset.

I rebuttoned my shirt, capturing the warm mess, straightened my tie, and soldiered on. I was determined to see the lesson through, despite my less-than-graceful display.

Later that evening, I shared my mishap with Mum. It left quite the impression. When she found herself feeling queasy during a glider experience months later, she snubbed the offered sick bag, invoked my name, declaring, "No need. I know what to do. My daughter's a pilot," before vomiting inside her own shirt.

Reflecting on my turbulent, shirt-soiling first lesson, I realised I faced a choice. With a year's flying lessons already paid upfront, do I throw in the towel, or grit my teeth and press on? I pressed on despite vomiting on the next 2 lessons! Eventually I tamed my fear and passed my Private Pilot Licence. Now I needed to fly solo hours to gain the experience to qualify as a Commercial Pilot.

Not content to fly up and down the East Coast of Australia repeatedly, I opted for the challenge of flying small, single-engine aircraft from USA to Australia—think a Hyundai Getz with wings. Typically, this is approximately 56 hours flying from the West Coast of the United States, over the Pacific Ocean, to the East Coast of Australia. It was impossible to do this in one continuous flight.

Small aircraft will typically fly for 5.5 hours with a range of up to 700nm. My longest leg on these flights was 2070nm - around 13.5 hours (if the winds were good), and the shortest was only 5 hours (again, with winds in my favour). I would need to 'Island Hop' across the Pacific and make capacity modifications to the small plane.

I wanted to be as prepared as possible, so I signed on for a 'training flight' with an experienced Ferry pilot. Our trip was from Ardmore, New Zealand across to Kempsey in Northern New South Wales,

Australia. Considering I would be ferrying small aircraft over much longer distances than this, coupled with stories of pilots who had ditched in the ocean, I needed further training. I opted for Helicopter Underwater Escape Training to help me survive if I had to ditch (land or crash), into the ocean. Despite this training, the impact of what I was about to do really hit home about a week before I left for the USA to fly a small plane solo across the Pacific. I was a 28-year-old single mum. The nightmares were intense. Regardless, I flew over to the United States and picked up the aircraft from Scottsdale, Arizona.

I conducted a couple of test flights in the area and encountered a situation with air traffic control poking fun at my Australian accent. This ribbing continued all the way to a small airport south of LAX, where, after landing, we shared a laugh at the communication difficulties despite speaking the same language.

In anticipation of the journey across the ocean, I made a series of modifications to the aircraft. One major task involved removing the rear seats and installing a 750kg rubber fuel tank so I could extend the range of this small plane. I added a manual hand pump to transfer fuel from the bladder to the wing. That was just the beginning of my problem-solving adventure. Confronted with concerns about oil consumption, I got creative. Feeling like a modern-day MacGyver, I devised a solution using a child's play syringe and plastic tubing. This makeshift oil replenishment system extended from the cockpit to the engine's oil filler cap, ensuring I could administer a steady supply of oil throughout the journey over the Pacific.

Aircraft modified; I was ready. I gathered other necessary equipment: Life Jacket, Life Raft, Axe, batteries for three hand-held GPS's, Flares, Chocolate, Sat phone, permits, food, water, and I set aside US$10,000 for any emergencies en route.

My first attempt ended early. Needing to turn back two hours into the flight due to my HF radio no longer working. I had tried to fake my way through San Francisco airspace, pretending I could hear their calls whilst I had them on another frequency. It didn't go down well. They threatened to scramble Airforce jets to escort me back (or shoot me down, I couldn't decipher which). I wasn't intentionally non-compliant, I was overweight for a landing, so I needed to burn fuel, time and therefore money, before it was safe and legal to land.

Rather than labelling the first attempt as a failure, I redefined it as a valuable, albeit costly, practice session. The following day, determined, I arrived at the airport bright and early, eager to embark on my second attempt at flying across the Pacific from the USA to Australia.

Navigating through San Francisco airspace, a sense of accomplishment washed over me. The air traffic controllers recognised me from the previous day and greeted my departure with a hint of relief, and grateful to see me continuing my journey.

The first leg was 13.5 hours from Hollister to Hilo (Hawaii). I had a fuel management plan. I would use the left-wing fuel tank till half empty, switch to the right wing, and hand pump furiously to refill the left and then switch back. I would repeat this until the bladder was empty, or the right wing, whichever came first. Each tank swap was a race against time. If the right wing ran out of fuel, so did I.

I hoped I had calculated enough fuel for reserves and the headwind. I was constantly listening and watching for any engine upset or splutter, ears straining for the slightest change in engine pitch. When I wasn't pumping fuel or syringing oil, I would be calculating my position relative to the huge charts that showed only blue ocean.

Interrupting my constant monitoring was entertaining chats on frequency 123.45. A channel for pilots to chat up in the air.

"Aircraft 6,500 feet, West of Monterey, do you read?" came the call.

"November 3576 Lima is 300 nautical miles west off Monterey. Maintaining 6,500. Go ahead," I replied.

"November 3576 Lima go numbers," they requested. "Numbers" means to tune the VHF radio to frequency 123.45.

"November 3576 Lima, on numbers," I called.

"What the hell are you flying?"

I told them.

"Where are you from?"

I told them.

"Where are you going?"

I told them.

"Are you fucking crazy?!?"

This happened a few times with commercial airlines overhead. Other pilots have since called me bonkers, mad, insane, crazy, and only occasionally mentioned I had 'big cajónes'. I did question my life choice many times.

Small planes don't have toilets. On the New Zealand training flight, the male pilot who was training me could conveniently wee into an empty juice bottle. I had to hold mine in for over 5 hours! It was the first and only time I would ferry a small plane with pants on.

For the Pacific Ocean crossing, I wore a skirt, and carried a Travel John. A few of them. A Travel John is a device that you can pee into, and like a nappy, it's filled with absorbent material that can hold a litre of liquid. I would kneel on the seat backwards, stretch out the Travel John, and be careful not to push the control column with my derriere, lest I dive into the ocean.

As my fuel burned, I navigated low clouds, rain, and strong winds, and after 12 hours I was approaching land. Legs numb, brain numb, dehydrated, and unfamiliar with the airspace. I wasn't in the best condition for an unfamiliar landing. Luckily, they understood my accent and carefully guided me into Hilo. I could barely walk when I stepped out of the aircraft, but was relieved my feet were finally feeling land.

The first leg of the Pacific crossing was over.

"Flying may not be all plain sailing, but the fun of it is worth the price" - Amelia Earhart

My journey's next stop was Kiribati. It was in this vicinity that rumours circulated about Amelia Earhart's disappearance and where her final flight is said to have ended. Unable to complete the leg from Lae in Papua New Guinea to Howland Island, just north of Kiribati, Amelia's disappearance remains one of aviation's greatest mysteries. Reflecting on her courageous tale offered me profound insight into the formidable obstacles she overcame, both technically and as a woman in a male-dominated field. This contemplation and appreciation of the trailblazers before me, served to rid lingering doubts I had harboured about my own crossing.

Arriving in Kiribati, I was greeted by a unique sight. No fences around the airport, and the runway teeming with red crabs.

I was told that if you must ditch, it is best to do so in US waters as their coast guard is amazing, rescuing you within 8-10 hours. But I was heading into international waters and wasn't confident my rescuers would be as timely as the US Coast Guard if something went wrong. The legs might be shorter, but the strain on my nerves much higher.

On the third day of my journey, I flew to Pago Pago, then Norfolk Island, intending to stay one night. A setback occurred when one of the engine pistons began to run rough, requiring me to extend for two nights. Fortunately, an aircraft engineer living on the island graciously helped. Although the prognosis initially appeared bleak, he managed to perform a makeshift repair that provided enough assurance to proceed to the mainland.

On one island, the US$10K came in handy when the price of fuel mysteriously increased (doubled)—most likely as it was my only option, and I wasn't a commercial airline.

My final legs were Lord Howe and then mainland Australia. I was nearly home.

I finally landed. I'd made it. I'd crossed the Pacific in a plane the size of a Hyundai Getz. I would soon see my son, and was building flight hours, but still not enough for my commercial licence. I needed a lot more, so… I did that trip twice more! Other pilots were now convinced I was crazy.

I didn't even get paid to fly these 'insane' crossings, but I was determined to build my hours and reach my goal.

The flights were harrowing, but when I touched down on Australian soil after that last flight, a profound sense of accomplishment washed over me. I had completed three flights across the Pacific and proved to myself I could do anything I set my mind to.

I was finally on the path to achieving my dream of becoming a commercial pilot.

My private pilot experience was invaluable as I transitioned into the commercial aviation realm. Despite further sexist attitudes and obstacles I faced along the way, I persevered, driven by a determination to defy expectations and prove my worth.

I obtained my Commercial Pilot Licence – I could now finally get paid. I ventured into instructing, guiding aspirants toward their own aviation dreams. My aspirations of becoming an Airline pilot were still the goal. However, more hours of experience were needed before I could apply.

Getting creative with how I would do this and needing to stay based in Sydney with my son and mum, I became a charter pilot. Flying across the continent and navigating the vast expanse of Australia's skies, every journey an encounter with diverse souls and unforeseen challenges. At the time, pilots were aplenty (shake a tree and 10 would fall to the ground), so airlines were upping their requirements to get the best of the best. Still needing 1500 hours to meet the minimum experience required, I took on flights often overlooked or shunned by other pilots – gritty assignments in dodgy aircraft, often in bad weather.

At times, the airline's minimum requirements seemed distant, particularly after enduring harrowing flights in adverse weather or facing judgmental passengers questioning the safety and skill of a female charter pilot. However, I made it. My work as a regional airline pilot was a stepping stone to "the majors", with every flight an adventure. These flights increased my resilience and gratitude.

The journey of a pilot transcends mere occupation – aviation fuel courses through our veins, becoming our very lifeblood. There's a joke among us: How do you know there's a pilot in the room? They'll tell you!

Saying yes when asked, even when unsure of how to accomplish the task, has been a guiding principle that has shaped my life. It's a lesson I learned early on, amidst the challenges and adventures of my aviation journey.

In the cockpit, there were moments when I was presented with unexpected requests or faced with daunting challenges. Navigating through treacherous weather conditions or troubleshooting mechanical issues mid-flight. There were times when doubt crept in, and the path forward seemed uncertain. In those pivotal moments, I made a conscious decision to embrace the unknown and respond with a resounding yes. I trusted in my abilities, my training, and my intuition, knowing that with determination and perseverance, I would find a way to overcome any obstacle that stood in my path. It pushed me out of my comfort zone, forcing me to grow and evolve both as a pilot and as a person.

Through these experiences, I learned the power of resilience, adaptability, and the importance of embracing uncertainty. I discovered that sometimes, the greatest rewards lie on the other side of fear, and that by saying yes to the unknown, we open ourselves up to endless possibilities and opportunities for growth.

As an airline captain, I flew millions of passengers, millions of miles, and to the captain who once questioned my capabilities, to the Careers Advisor who dismissed my aspirations, and to all the doubters along the way, I reiterate: women don't make good Captains; we make great Captains.

Epilogue

For the full story of my countless exhilarating and nerve-wracking experiences, such as navigating through storms without instrumentation post-lightning strike, serving as the personal pilot for a globally renowned musician, and dealing with unruly passengers who threw bottles of urine during a flight, read my memoir "Keep Going Until You Can't".

Stay updated on the book's launch through the link: https://www.michellehuntington.com/author

MICHELLE HUNTINGTON

Inspirational Keynote Speaker, Leadership Coach, Podcast Host, Corporate Trainer, and Media Commentator

https://esys.io/s/michelle-huntington

Heather Disher
Multifaceted Business Owner with Energy and Heart

ABOUT THE AUTHOR: HEATHER DISHER

As a young teen, I made a very adult decision - I chose to live as a survivor and not a victim of bullying. Since then, I have made many other big decisions, like moving countries, taking on roles in completely unfamiliar industries, starting a business, and writing a chapter in this book. Regardless of the journey, I have chosen to share what I've learned, empower others, and lead with my values and purpose.

Today, I am a multifaceted dual business owner, advisor, and director, and I hold the position of Chair on both Governance and Advisory Boards. I provide advice and solutions to business owners as they overcome challenges and bring their ideas to life. My diverse career has spanned multiple sectors, locations, and business sizes, allowing me to offer unique insights and benefits to individuals and organisations.

I find joy in helping others achieve their dreams. I love working with and empowering CEOs, visionaries, business owners, and leaders responsible for their business's success. My clients tell me they love my unique style of asking the right questions blended with curiosity, energy, and passion.

In my spare time, I enjoy running and outdoor exploration with my dog Koda or volunteering.

CHAPTER 5

MY LEADERSHIP JOURNEY

By Heather Disher

I spent my childhood trying to be invisible, as small and as nothing as possible. I'm a survivor of bullying and abuse.

Every day of my primary school years, I was physically and mentally bullied by a group of girls. There was no one that would stand up for me because if they did, the energy would shift to them. I was on my own—not even the teachers stood up for me.

It wasn't until I was nearly 14 years old that my emotions overpowered me, and I had a breakdown.

It was a normal day, except it wasn't a school day. I remember being able to breathe a little easier, knowing I didn't have to navigate the school environment. My family was talking about an upcoming school activity I didn't want to attend. My grandmother was advocating for me, and as the voices got louder, I could feel myself sinking…

My vision blurred and sound retreated. I could no longer feel my body, and my mind was blank and at peace. A moment later, I panicked. I couldn't breathe; I was shutting down, and it was ok; the blackness was calming, and the panic drifted away. I was safe. In my darkness, I noticed a tiny but very bright spark. It was like those party sparklers but smaller; it was so pretty. It was getting more colourful and bigger, lighting the dark, still small but bright. I remember feeling happiness creep in. I knew at that moment this was a piece of me, a tiny spark.

I had a choice to make—live or die. Stay in the dark or step up and claim my spark.

I claimed my spark and took a breath and then another until I could open my eyes. I found myself on the floor with concerned faces looking at me, expressing their worry and reassurance that everything would be okay. I don't recall much about the rest of the day except that I needed to rest.

From that day on, I stood up to my bullies; I chose to stand and fight, to never again choose invisibility. I may have built walls and taken hits, but I knew I wanted more for myself. I wanted to feel safe, to be seen, to be valued, and because I wanted this, I wanted to give this to others.

Today my spark is strong and vibrant, and little did I know that that horrible, painful day when my world went black was the first step on my journey to being the leader I am today. I want to share with you my journey of choice, where I went wrong and right, how I made peace with errors, and my ongoing learning path.

I started full-time employment a few months before my 18th birthday. I had a burning need to start my life on my terms. My first job was as a receptionist. I found I could hear what people were saying—not just the words, but hear their needs. Being able to listen well and then deliver aligned outcomes placed me on a constant promotion track. I moved through the areas of the business, and within two years, I outgrew the business.

By the time I turned 20, I had become aware of how people outgrow their roles, purpose, and values in a business. This awareness was the fuel for my business today.

I had gone from a small office of 6 people that delivered national radio advertising solutions to an advertising agency that would later merge and become one of the world's largest. I was organised, focused, reliable and competent, and I continued to learn.

I noticed that others weren't sharing as much as I was. While I was sharing what I was learning and trying to inspire and provide opportunities for others, they were not doing the same. The little girl inside me who yearns to be noticed wanted to ensure that others were also seen and heard. I realized that by teaching others, they would be able to handle some of my workload, allowing me to learn new things. I wasn't just learning by sharing, but also through delegating tasks and empowering others.

Outwardly, I appeared to be thriving. However, internally, I was still battling a strong conflict. Professionally, I was making progress and achieving great results, but personally, I was still hiding. I was attempting to change, not only myself but also the people around me. I recall thinking, "If you shared with me, we could make this business even better together." However, in contrast, I decided to increase my sharing of knowledge, and at times, I came across as a 'know-it-all'.

The downside of sharing is that it can sometimes backfire. Some people took my ideas and used them to promote themselves. I had a choice to either fight against the injustice or to reflect on what I wanted and why I wanted to share. This reflective thinking has become one of my greatest strengths, both personally and professionally. A leader needs to be able to consider issues from various angles. We can't fully understand a problem or find a solution unless we examine it from different perspectives.

It was during this time that I assumed my first official professional leadership role. Like all developing leaders, I made mistakes along the way. One of my biggest regrets was holding back a member of my team. This individual was very enthusiastic and committed to her goals, but I hindered her progress by constantly providing examples of how certain approaches had failed in the past. In hindsight, I realise I was discouraging her empowerment, which is something that deeply saddens me. The more she sought my help to move forward, the more I found myself trying to shield her from taking risks.

I realised it was time for me to leave. I couldn't hold back myself for anyone else. I had started in this role as the sole employee and built the business into a success. Stepping away was hard, but it was the right decision.

I spent the next few years pondering my purpose while working internationally. In a different country and in an industry I knew nothing about, surrounded by people I didn't know. I was working in the technology industry, specifically the creation of search algorithms for intranet (this was before Google; it was a strange and fascinating world). It was the dot.com boom and everywhere I turned, there was something new to learn and understand. It was a test of my courage. I made the decision to do this not only to expand my learning but also to start a new chapter in my life.

It wasn't until years later that I realised moving wasn't the way to start anew. The change I sought was within me, not in my location, but that's a whole other story. I found it a bit challenging to make friends outside of work. As a bullying survivor, I had trouble with trust and creating connections, but within the workplace, I was open, honest, and transparent. I enjoyed sharing my knowledge and helping others. Over the next few years, I found myself becoming a leader. People started seeking to be part of my team, even those I hadn't worked with before.

By 2000, I was leading a global team for a bespoke search algorithm solutions firm, working with some of the world's largest companies. I attracted people to join my team because they wanted to be part of something and work with a leader who empowered them. My leadership style, which was based on trust, support, and accountability, was natural to me. I was an effective leader, even though I didn't realize it at the time. Looking back, I find it amusing to realize that I was often labelled as "the youngest," "the first woman," "handling the biggest contract," "the first Australian" – you get the idea.

What I am most proud of is the way I connected with people. As a survivor, being vulnerable with others can be very difficult.

I had incredible talent in my team; we all had different skills. Understanding each other and supporting each other wasn't easy, so I made a choice to share my idea – or what I would later learn was my vision – with my team. I did this for each project and client. I ensured my team had the resources and support they needed to be empowered to deliver, and deliver we did. When we didn't or something went wrong, I took responsibility; I never once blamed my team.

Take a moment and think about a time that you were awesome and didn't know it – go on, take a moment to stop reading and travel through your memory.

Now, when you find that time, I want you to compare that moment to today – can you see how much further you have come or maybe you can see some steps you can take as you develop on your leadership journey? Write down your thoughts and know this – I believe in you – why? Because you are reading my story.

So, back to my learning. While traveling the world and meeting many important people, I realised my energy was getting depleted. It took me some time to understand that I was an introvert. Although I was working with and leading hundreds of people, I found I needed a quiet, people-free space to regain my energy.

When your energy dips and stays low, your character becomes strained, and as a leader, some unpleasant traits can emerge. I wasn't as patient or empathetic as I normally was. This created small problems that grew into something bigger. For example, when I was really tired, I didn't hear or listen well, so I missed important information about how a person was feeling or the impacts of delays on a project. The results include mediocre outcomes. People want and need to feel heard and seen. I know this, and yet I let myself dip into that person who didn't listen well or was too rushed to really hear what was being said. It was time to take a break and reset.

Taking care of myself, getting some rest, and being able to reset was a blessing. I was leading a merger between the UK company I worked for and a US firm while still delivering global solutions. Being clear-headed and having a great team was a winning combination.

Talking through the 'why', the 'how', and potential variables involved in this merger were a critical part of this successful transition, as was the power of clear and honest communication, sharing the vision, and being transparent about the process.

Merging businesses is about systems, customers and aligning the multitude of resources. More importantly it is about the people. This level of change can be scary especially during the dotcom era. Some people lost their jobs; others were being forced to evolve and change to represent the new. None of this was easy.

As a person who embraces change, I would learn that I was an innovator—someone who loves the why and how of things. It was a privilege to lead the business through that change and to guide so many people into their "new."

After the merger was finalised, I was responsible for assembling the teams to manage operations in North America and for finding a new leader for this team. As I conducted evaluations and recruitment, I observed that many recruitment agencies used a "tick box" system. If candidates didn't fit into the predetermined categories, they were often overlooked. This made me concerned about how this new information would affect my own situation, but I knew I would have to address that later.

I was working in an industry that was paving the way for the future, but because of the faulty recruitment system, I struggled to find the right people to join our team. Despite reaching out to everyone I knew, making numerous phone calls and sending countless emails, I couldn't seem to find people with the specific skills and mindset we needed. It took much longer than anticipated, but eventually, I was able to assemble an exceptional team and found an excellent leader for them. It required unconventional thinking to achieve this.

I see being able to replace myself as a sign of my success as a leader. I believe that if someone else can step in and take over from me without issue, I have done a great job. I've replaced myself so many times over the years in so many different roles and I needed to do it again.

After returning to Australia and taking a month or so to rest and recover, I encountered a problem. Despite submitting over 100 job applications, each of which was personalised to showcase my fit for the role and what I could contribute, the recruitment system's tick-box approach failed to recognise how my experience could contribute to growth, transformation, and international expansion.

After establishing connections within my network, I secured a short-term contract with an Australian company. Although the company was small, it had ambitious plans to expand internationally. Using my prior experience to benefit small and medium enterprises was incredibly fulfilling.

Previously, my career had been primarily focused on B2B (Business-to-Business) environments. However, fuelled by my newfound passion for supporting the growth of SMEs, I embraced a new role in the emerging market of adult education, which belonged to a B2C (Business-to-Consumer) company.

Leading with purpose and transparency, my success within the B2C sector flourished. This led to numerous opportunities to return to the B2B sector, and I found myself becoming an advisor to Governance Boards, providing guidance and solutions through inquiries and considerations.

With the range of contract opportunities available, I decided it was time to start my own firm and become a business owner. In the first 6-12 months, I took on several projects that were not the right fit for me in terms of value alignment and expectations. The more I learnt about where I could deliver well, the more I was able to turn away business. At the time, it was uncommon for someone to turn down business because it wasn't the right fit. I noticed that I surprised some of my peers, while others were curious about what I was doing and why it was all so different.

If you find yourself in this situation, I offer you two tips.

1. If you are the person at the forefront of change, I encourage you to get some good people around you and I'm not talking yes or like-minded people. Find people to challenge your reasoning.
2. If you are working with a person at the forefront of change, then be curious. Ask them questions. Learn how they think. Find ways to support or challenge them. Choose to be part of the future.

I was working with SMEs on strategy, growth mindset and plans to take them into their future. I was supporting the dreams of founders, and I loved it!

I've been applying the lessons from my past to my current situation, and it hasn't been easy. Even simple tasks like pricing a quote are challenging when there's no benchmark to reference. How do you determine your value? How can you use profit to grow your business when you don't have a year's worth of earnings in the bank as a safety net?

I overcame these and many other obstacles to achieve success.

I noticed that funding and capital were extremely challenging when working with many SMEs. I became knowledgeable about finance and financial and capital markets.

During that time, it seemed like the logical next step for me was to explore venture capital. I was providing management consulting services and had the ability to manage a business, so I felt that combining investment and management was a perfect fit for me.

However, I soon found myself stretched to my limits. The workload was unsustainable despite the many opportunities I could see. I ended up purchasing a business with a partner and taking on the role of running it, which also required me to move to a different state. Balancing running two businesses, managing numerous opportunities and contracts, being away from friends and family, and working around the clock took a toll on me.

After feeling exhausted and unable to keep up, the businesses began to struggle. Eventually, I made the decision to return home to find a solution for the two failing businesses. I ended up selling one and closing the other.

Reflecting on this period, I realised that I couldn't handle everything on my own. I needed a team or individuals whom I could trust and delegate responsibilities to. Being bogged down in day-to-day tasks hindered my strategic abilities, increased stress, and tested my resilience. As a leader, it's important to recognise where and how you can do your best work.

During a period of international expansion, I offered my expertise to an organisation in its early stages of growth, reigniting my passion for supporting small and medium-sized enterprises (SMEs). This led me to join the board of a not-for-profit, marking the beginning of my journey into governance leadership.

As I travelled between the US and Australia, I realised I was neglecting my personal connections due to work commitments. I had to make a choice: either stop and reset or continue until I burned out.

Recognising the importance of self-care for effective leadership, I decided to prioritise my well-being. After working in ladies' fashion retail for about a year, I focused on rebuilding my energy levels, improving my health, and expanding my knowledge of governance. I then ventured into a new sector where I had no prior experience.

Working with a family-owned business presented its own set of challenges and successes. Communication of a clear vision was essential for garnering support and effective leadership.

During this time, I also expanded my governance skills by taking on roles on two different boards.

Meeting an entrepreneur led to a significant personal change for me. I transitioned into the role of an Integrator in a virtual business, where I was responsible for turning the owner's vision into reality. This role allowed me to optimise and grow the business, and it was a pivotal point in my life. The support I received from this entrepreneur helped me overcome barriers from my early years.

Prior to the COVID-19 pandemic, I had already experienced remote work for at least six years. However, the demands during the pandemic led to a lack of innovation within the team, resulting in a decline in the business.

Recognising this failure on my part, I focused on strategising and reorganising, creating opportunities for growth. I learned from my mistakes, understanding that failure is inevitable, provided I learn from it.

I encountered challenges in finding committed team members for a virtual business. To address this, I established a company to source talent.

Today, I am the owner of two businesses, Alchemy Outsourcing and Disher Advisory Synergy, both built on the principles of giving and receiving, accountability, and empowerment. I continue to share my experiences, emphasising the importance of learning, openness, curiosity, and courage.

Finally, I hope my story inspires you to embrace imperfection, strive for personal and professional growth, and extend kindness and patience to yourself. You are enough, and you are fabulous!

I invite you to reach out and share your story with me or discuss any aspect of my journey that resonates with you. Let's connect and continue to create a positive impact.

HEATHER DISHER

Multifaceted Business Owner with Energy and Heart

https://esys.io/s/heather-disher

Polina Kesov
Drawing from Personal Adversity to Offer Unmatched Support and Guidance to Business Owners

ABOUT THE AUTHOR: POLINA KESOV

My name is Polina Kesov, and I am an accomplished insurance broker with an ongoing commitment to providing exceptional service and tailored solutions to my clients. With a profound understanding of the insurance industry and a dedication to staying abreast of the latest trends and regulations, I offer expert advice and guidance to individuals and businesses in need of the right coverage.

Based in Sydney CBD, ii-A is not merely my business—it's my passion. For over 18 years, my team and I have treated our clients like family, taking a personal approach to insurance. We take the time to understand our clients and their unique needs, enabling us to offer bespoke solutions that genuinely meet their requirements. Our focus is on building long-term relationships grounded in trust, reliability, and exceptional service.

Our extensive knowledge of the insurance market allows us to adeptly navigate the complexities of policies and coverage options, ensuring our clients receive the best possible protection. Whether it's personal insurance, business insurance, or specialised coverage, we possess the expertise to guide you through the process and identify the most suitable policies.

At ii-A, we recognise that every client is unique, and we invest the time to listen and comprehend their specific circumstances. This meticulous attention to detail empowers us to craft insurance solutions that are not only effective but also aligned with our clients' goals and aspirations. We are dedicated to providing continuous support and advice, assisting our clients in making informed decisions and adapting to any changes in their insurance needs.

As I often say, "Action speaks louder than words," so I invite you to contact me today to discover how we can assist you.

I am also passionate about sharing my personal journey of overcoming adversities. These experiences enable me to connect deeply with other business owners, offering not only my expertise as their insurance broker but also my support as someone who listens, understands, and provides valuable suggestions and guidance.

CHAPTER 6

UNSTOPPABLE RESILIENCE: MY JOURNEY OF COURAGE

By Polina Kesov

In the enchanting city of Odessa, Ukraine, my early years unfolded like a vivid tapestry woven with threads of love and wisdom by my family. My upbringing was deeply rooted in values taught by my parents and grandparents—bravery, empathy, resilience, love, and compassion. These virtues laid the groundwork for my life, highlighting the importance of forming genuine connections.

I was the only child of my devoted parents. While they worked tirelessly to brighten my future, much of my upbringing was in the caring hands of my maternal grandparents. From a young age, I observed my parents' relentless efforts in their business, striving to forge a better life for our family. Their determination and hard work are deeply ingrained in my DNA, providing a solid foundation that has shaped who I am today.

My mother and I often reflect on how their efforts, made over four decades ago, continue to yield benefits—not just for me, but for my children and potentially for generations to come. It's a powerful reminder that hard work is never in vain. Every experience and every person we encounter teaches us valuable lessons and contributes to our journey in meaningful ways.

The 1990s brought sweeping cultural and economic shifts to Ukraine, a period marked by my family's bold decision to seek a new life in Sydney, Australia, amidst the tumult of my parents' divorce. My mother faced the challenges of my parents' divorce with strength and resilience. Immigrating into the unknown was a leap filled with challenges, but also rich with possibilities, paving the way for a hopeful new chapter and boundless opportunities.

Upon our arrival in Australia, I was determined to embrace this new beginning fully. I threw myself into integrating into the vibrant Australian culture, completing my education at one of Sydney's most prestigious schools. Here, I forged lasting friendships and focused on mastering English, driven by a desire to make a meaningful impact, and not just be seen as an outsider.

Although I was surrounded by many from my cultural background, I found myself deeply intrigued by the Australian way of life.

Life in Australia was exhilarating, filled with new experiences and opportunities for growth every day. After graduating from high school, I completed beauty therapy college, where I honed my skills in enhancing people's beauty and happiness. It was here that I discovered my passion for people and helping others. At the time, I didn't realise each step was laying the foundation for my future.

After gaining experience in prestigious beauty salons in Sydney's Eastern Suburbs, I decided to pursue my entrepreneurial ambitions by starting my own business.

At the tender age of 19, I founded Alpha and Omega Beauty, an elegant salon along the iconic Bondi Beach. Despite facing scepticism due to my youth, my unwavering determination propelled me forward.

I remember walking into a real estate agency, requesting a contract for an empty shop. I was told I was too young, but I was able to explain that age is irrelevant when the desire to succeed is bigger. The shop was leased to me with very favourable rates because the real estate agent was impressed by my determination and approach.

Around the same time, I embraced two other significant life roles— I got married and embraced motherhood. Becoming a mother at 19 brought its own set of challenges, but with the mindset of "I will make it work, no matter what," I navigated the complexities of balancing a new business and a new life.

The birth of my first son marked a period of personal growth and instilled in me a deeper level of resilience and strength. Raising a child as a very young mother was initially confronting, but his wellbeing became my top priority. At that time, my husband was a university student and working part-time to ensure our family had everything we needed. My family supported me, teaching me everything about motherhood. I envisioned my son's life and the achievements he would have. I knew that by staying focused, I could raise a child who was just as determined and resilient as I am. Now, as I look at him, he is my joy and pride.

My husband often jokes that we were growing up alongside our son because we were such young parents. He also frequently reminds me that, despite my youth, I faced every challenge fearlessly and with a positive mindset.

Life, however, had more challenges in store. Just as my business began to flourish after several years at the same location, I received a demolition notice for the salon premises, which meant I would need to relocate. Instead of viewing this as a setback, I saw it as an opportunity to reinvent myself once again.

I remember having a cup of tea at my favourite coffee shop next to my salon, reflecting on my life and my reasons for being in business. I love writing things down when I think or discuss them with someone I trust, but that day, I wanted to reflect on my own, without any outside influence. I like visualising things, so I thought about my roles as a wife, mother, daughter, and granddaughter, as well as my role as a business owner. I realised that my "why" is my family—their life and their future. Deep down, I knew beauty therapy wasn't fulfilling enough for me. Perhaps I needed this moment to push me towards making changes and exploring what else life has to offer.

I chose to leave the beauty industry and venture into the world of general insurance, a field completely unfamiliar to me at the time. There wasn't a specific reason for going into this industry, but it has turned out to be one of the best decisions I've made in my life.

This career shift was more than a means of survival; it was an opportunity to excel in a new arena. I rapidly ascended through the ranks of the insurance industry, acquiring essential skills and knowledge that would prove invaluable. I pursued all necessary qualifications with diligence, ensuring that I was not just competent, but exceptional in my role.

I was fortunate to secure a role at one of the world's leading insurance companies, and I found this job personally fulfilling. Helping people in need and providing valuable service ignited my passion for the job and boosted my career prospects.

During this time, I welcomed my second son, whose arrival further fuelled my determination to provide a prosperous future for my family. Although my sons are six years apart, I often watch their interactions now that they are both adults with their achievements, and I feel truly blessed. They are very close and very supportive of each other, as well as overprotective.

I believe my upbringing and resilience have shaped who they are today, and I eagerly anticipate their bright futures. They have adopted the same mindset: "I will make it work, no matter what."

One day at the office, my manager shared a poignant reflection. Battling illness, he expressed deep regrets about missed opportunities in his life. He advised me earnestly: "Polina, always remember, when an opportunity arises, conquer it! You can always return if it doesn't pan out, but if you never try, that door may close forever."

Years later, his words still resonate with me. I find myself continually evaluating each opportunity that arises—be it in my personal life or business—viewing each as a potential gateway to explore. This approach has consistently guided me successfully through numerous decisions and remains a foundational principle in my journey.

My journey took a profound turn when I re-entered the entrepreneurial world with a close friend, launching ii-A, an insurance brokerage firm, during the Global Financial Crisis. This venture was not just a business but a testament to our resilience and belief in facing adversity head-on. We started from scratch, securing an Australian Financial Services Licence, and setting up our first office in Sydney's CBD. Our client-focused approach led to high retention rates of clients and a growing reputation in the industry.

However, life throws its harshest curveball yet after 17 years of a very successful business venture, when my business partner, also my best friend, was diagnosed with incurable cancer. His untimely death plunged me into profound grief and emotions I had never experienced before. This period tested every fibre of my being, making the mantra "what does not kill us makes us stronger" more relevant than ever.

Despite these trials, I pushed forward, making strategic decisions that not only kept the business afloat but also allowed it to thrive. During this time, I realised that we often limit ourselves to our fears. Someone recently remarked that I seem like a different person now, full of confidence and ease. I responded, "I wish someone had told me earlier that most problems are fears we don't need to have and that we are stronger than we believe."

Having a supportive network and maintaining a positive mindset is crucial. Additionally, practicing daily gratitude is important because we have so much to be thankful for, even when life seems challenging. I thank God for my trials and for guiding me through the various moments in my life. His guidance has been my strength, helping me navigate every challenge and triumph.

My family's unwavering support, along with the dedication of my team, played crucial roles in navigating these turbulent times.

Recalling those days still stirs deep emotions. Critics doubted my ability to run the business alone, claiming the "business brain" was gone and dismissing me as merely a "pretty face." These painful accusations could have overwhelmed me, but instead, they ignited my determination to prove them wrong, driven by my conviction that their doubts were based on unwarranted emotions.

Many suggested that as a woman, I could not thrive in a male-dominated industry. People tried to step into the business, seeing an opportunity in my vulnerability. However, this only strengthened my resolve to demonstrate my foundational role in ii-A from the outset, particularly in a business where relationships are key to growth and success.

During that time of profound grief, loss, and uncertainty, I discovered my inner strength, and many aspects of life took on a completely different meaning.

While I can't change the past, these experiences have taught me invaluable lessons, compelling me to share and emphasise that persistence can overcome any obstacle.

I deeply wish I could tell my late business partner now that I cherish the beautiful moments we shared and am grateful for every lesson learned. His untimely departure was a tragedy, but in his memory, I strive to lead a meaningful life and inspire others to make a difference. Ultimately, we should be remembered not for our achievements alone but for the love we share.

As I reflect on my journey, I am reminded of the importance of resilience, the power of adaptability, and the strength that comes from overcoming adversity. My story is one of continual growth and transformation, not just in business but in personal development. Through it all, I have learned that life is not just about facing challenges but about transforming them into stepping stones for success.

Now, as I stand ready to embark on the next chapter of my life, I carry with me the lessons learned and the strength gained from each experience. My mission remains clear—to serve and help others, striving to make my mark in the insurance industry and beyond, driven by a purpose of freedom and the pursuit of changing lives. I return to my roots and the values my grandparents taught me: bravery, empathy, resilience, love, and compassion. It's interesting how, later in life, you come to realise the importance of these values. I now stand firmly by each one.

As I continue to reflect on the adversities and triumphs, I am guided by a renewed purpose to serve as a beacon of resilience and determination. My business, ii-A, has not just survived but has become a symbol of integrity and excellence within the insurance industry. We have nurtured relationships with clients who see us not just as brokers but as trusted advisors, helping them to navigate the complexities of risk and protection.

Our approach has always been deeply relational. We believe in the power of connection—not just as a business strategy but as a cornerstone of our practice. This has allowed us to maintain a high client retention rate, with many of our clients having been with us since the very beginning. Our dedication to our client's needs and our commitment to honest, personalised service are the pillars upon which we have built our reputation.

Amidst the growth and success, the loss of my business partner was a pivotal moment that forced me to reassess not just my business strategies but my values and resilience. His passing left a void, not just in the logistics of running our company but in the emotional landscape of my life. It taught me that resilience is not just about enduring pain but also about navigating the complexities of human emotions and relationships.

From this experience, I learned the importance of clear communication and the necessity of establishing boundaries. These lessons reshaped our business practices and deepened my understanding of leadership. I realised that to lead effectively, one must not only manage a business's operations but also its soul—the people who bring it to life.

This realisation was transformative. I began to focus more on my team, investing in their growth and well-being. Our office became a space where open dialogue about challenges and successes was encouraged, fostering a culture of support and continuous improvement.

Moreover, this period of transformation pushed me to advocate for greater diversity and inclusion within the industry, as well as for women in business overall. Recognising the unique challenges faced by women in leadership, especially in traditionally male-dominated sectors like insurance, I became actively involved in mentoring other business professionals. By sharing my journey and the lessons I've learned, I hope to inspire others to pursue their ambitions fearlessly, regardless of the obstacles they might encounter.

Today, as I look to the future, I am excited about the possibilities that lie ahead.

Reflecting on my journey, I see it as more than just a tale of overcoming obstacles; it is a testament to the human spirit's ability to turn challenges into opportunities for growth. I hope my story inspires others to understand that resilience is not inherent but developed through experiences, choices, and the support of those around us. Life is full of changes—whether it's a career shift or adapting to a new culture after moving countries. Regardless of the path you take, stay positive and envision an amazing future because you have the power to create change.

As I continue to write new chapters in my life and career, I remain dedicated to my mission of making a positive impact in the lives of others. Whether through my business or my business community engagements, I strive to embody the principles of service, integrity, and perseverance. My story, "Unstoppable Resilience: My Journey of Courage," is far from over; it is continually evolving, guided by the lessons of the past and the promise of the future.

The personal trials I've endured have imbued me with an empathy that permeates every aspect of our business. Understanding the pain points of others, whether they are navigating the grief of loss or the stress of starting a new venture, allows us to not just meet their needs but to connect with them on a human level. This empathetic approach is what sets ii-A apart in a competitive industry.

As I reflect on my journey, from the challenges of a young immigrant adjusting to a new country to navigating the complexities of entrepreneurship and personal loss, I see a mosaic of experiences that have shaped not only the business leader I have become but also the person I am today. These experiences have strengthened my resolve to use my platform not just for business success but as a force for good.

To those who are on their journeys, facing their own set of challenges, my message is one of hope and perseverance. The road may be long and fraught with obstacles, but it is also lined with opportunities to learn, grow, and redefine what is possible. Just as I have transformed each challenge into a stepping stone for success, I encourage others to embrace their struggles and see them as opportunities for personal and professional growth.

My journey of resilience and transformation continues, as vibrant and promising as the day it began. With each new challenge, I am reminded of how far I have come and how much further I aspire to go. I am excited to lead ii-A into the next chapter of its story, one that I hope will inspire current and future generations to pursue their visions with the same unrelenting drive and resilience that have guided me throughout my life. The path ahead is open and filled with potential, and I am ready to continue walking it with courage, passion, and unwavering determination.

While my story may seem modest compared to others, I hope it resonates with those who need encouragement. My experiences have shaped me into someone deeply committed to supporting others. For those who know me, it's clear that service is not just an activity, but my calling—it's integral to who I am and vital for fulfilling my life's vision and purpose.

If you're seeking guidance or support, I'm here to help. Whether you're dealing with professional challenges or personal hurdles, don't hesitate to reach out. Together, we can find ways to navigate your path forward. Let's connect and make your journey one of growth and success. Instead of worrying about what you cannot control, focus your energy on what you can create. This approach has helped me throughout my journey, and I hope my message makes a difference for at least one person in the world.

POLINA KESOV

Drawing from Personal Adversity to Offer Unmatched Support and Guidance to Business Owners

https://esys.io/s/polina-kesov

Jo Cooper
Warrior for Change

ABOUT THE AUTHOR: JO COOPER

Jo Cooper, a relentless Warrior for Change, fearlessly challenges the status quo, undaunted by backlash. She believes in the transformative Power of Your Voice to instigate social impact and sculpt a world free from bullying, abuse, and bystander culture. Jo's conviction in leadership is summed up in her words: "HATERS DON'T HESITATE, LOVERS STAY SILENT, AND BYSTANDERS HOLD ALL THE POWER."

Jo's passion for music emerged early, driving her to leave corporate project management to pursue her dreams as an artist. Her journey was marked by a pivotal moment: a harrowing experience in a violent relationship left her battered and alone, revealing the power of bystanders. Undeterred, Jo challenged the status quo again in a landmark legal battle in the New South Wales Supreme Court of Appeal In Australia, defending property and pet rights and securing a unanimous victory.

Now, combining advocacy with music, Jo educates and inspires corporations and communities to shift from bystander to proactive cultures, fostering social impact and unity while thwarting legal disputes. Her ultimate goal remains disempowering bullies and abusers through the harmonious chorus of collective voices.

Jo Cooper Instagram - https://www.instagram.com/jocoopermusic/

The Good Warrior - https://thegoodwarrior.com.au

CHAPTER 7

THE GOOD WARRIOR: FIGHTING FOR JUSTICE AND EQUALITY

By Jo Cooper

There are threads woven with moments that define us, moments that challenge the core of who we are, testing our values, tenacity, strength of character, and resilience. These moments are not just personal trials but calls to action and invitations to stand up and make a real impact.

I was the oldest of four girls in a first-generation Australian household. My father hailed from Sudan, while my mother came from Egypt. Describing our daily cultural dance as a test of negotiation, tenacity, and fiery passion would be an understatement; I'm convinced this is where my resilience was cemented. My younger self would be shocked to realise that I am truly my father's daughter, a fact I didn't fully appreciate at the time. The constant 'No because I said so' was never sufficient for me to accept; I was a perpetual challenge for my parents. Coming from a culture where men held control and women had less autonomy led to frustrating times for all of us.

To add to the mix, my heart was set on a dream: to become a singer/actress, weaving tales that could reshape the world. Everywhere we ventured, I'd unleash my voice, each stranger's praise kindling my spirit, though my father became increasingly vexed. Yet, for me, every compliment was a symphony of validation. This aspiration stood in stark contrast to the esteemed paths of lawyer or doctor that would have swelled my parents' hearts with pride.

The clash of cultures did not make us feel any less loved and blessed. We had a roof over our heads and food on our table, although many nights I would be sent to my room as I wasn't a fan of certain foods, and my dad was not going to entertain me insisting on a different meal—that's a whole other story. I have always been curious, asking why the moon shone and where the sun went… Everything intrigued me; I wanted to know how everything came to be.

After much chatter, my uncle often challenged me to be silent for an hour in exchange for $10; I would go into my room and silently interview myself with my hairbrush in the mirror. I'd ask myself all the questions I was curious about; goodness knows the answers. Then, I would collect that $10 and put it in my savings box. I was saving for my future early. I always felt like an old soul with a crazy, fun spirit, a typical Gemini. I remember the day I saw a pair of running shoes. I desperately wanted them, but my father said no. Little did I know he had left his job. He turned to me and said, "If you want them, go and earn them yourself." When we returned home from the store, I immediately walked the streets to find a job, which I found at our local fruit shop, I started work the very next day.

My father was furious when, at the end of the week, trying to hide a little smug smile on my face, I asked him to drive me back to the store to buy those shoes. He wasn't exactly pleased, but he still found it somewhat impressive. He would have loved for me to leave that job as I had made my point.

I loved the freedom of earning my own money, though, so I refused to give it up, much to his dismay. I told you I was my father's daughter! I met my first boyfriend while working at this job. However, it had to remain a secret because, in our culture, the norm is to get engaged and married. There's no concept of having a 'boyfriend,' as it's immediately associated with having lost one's virginity. The shame, guilt, and fear that accompany this are indescribable. Shame seemed far more daunting than death itself.

I remember the night my parents found out. I had told them I had to work late at the fruit shop. My father happened to drive past the fruit shop and noticed it was closed. He went door to door, looking for me at any of the friends' houses he knew of. When I finally appeared at home, it was like a funeral, but not the celebration of life kind. I'm talking about the ones where they wail and scream, and everything is BLACK. It wasn't merely frightening; it was bone-chilling, a moment that seized me with sheer terror. Even now, I can still feel the pounding of my heart, one of the few instances where genuine fear enveloped me, for not much else could shake me to my core.

I remember my father looming over me and saying, "I forbid you having a boyfriend." Now, me being me, this was an invitation to a tango of challenge, an irresistible call to test my mettle and dance with adversity. I can now say that I wholeheartedly wished I'd listened at that very moment. Both our parents disapproved of this relationship.

This relationship marked the onset of my first excruciating chapter, imprinting the significance of bystanders in my consciousness. After my father died suddenly from a stroke in Melbourne, I was in total shock and didn't allow it to sink in; I had to be strong for my mum and sisters. I remember being on the plane coming back home to Sydney, and all I could think of was that I had spent many years arguing with my dad over this boy; what wasted time.

The very next day, I broke up with him. This concluded in a violent rupture, relegating me to a hospital bed, tending to both physical and emotional wounds. I didn't have time to grieve my dad; I couldn't stop thinking about how cowardly this act was on many levels. He hadn't laid a hand on me before; why now? I found myself clinging to the exterior of a speeding vehicle, his vice-like grip encircling my wrist until he flung me aside as if I were a mere ragdoll.

As I lay there, battered and shattered, my dress shredded, all I saw was a sea of apathetic eyes. Not a single soul extended a helping hand or even asked me if I was okay. It was a surreal moment where the glaring absence of concern overshadowed the agony I had just endured. I felt insignificant, blood running down the side of my body, my skin mixed with bitumen. Under ordinary circumstances, I would have collapsed just from the sight of blood, yet it seemed inconsequential as my bewildered eyes scanned the indifferent onlookers. The mix of embarrassment and blame, how could I allow myself to be in this situation? and that small wish: I wish my dad were here to save me, was simultaneously rushing through my mind and heart.

I knew how I would have reacted if I had just witnessed what happened; I would have rushed to aid without hesitation. How could these bystanders bear witness to such a shocking ordeal and remain rooted in place, mere spectators to my suffering? I always had a strong sense of justice. Dad had a very stringent set of values, and although I didn't appreciate the description of justice, I knew the feeling deep in my DNA. I thought everyone looked out for one another. As someone deeply attuned to notions of justice, I grappled with many conflicting emotions. My long-time partner had treated me as though I were inconsequential, while strangers chose passivity over intervention. Why didn't something deep inside them scream out against a young girl being hurt so badly?

Fast-forward many years, and I faced another defining moment: a seemingly innocuous email sent on a July day in 2015. It started with a simple inquiry, a question veiled in curiosity about submitting a motion to change a by-law. Little did I know that this single email would herald a six-and-a-half-year odyssey, challenging me in ways I could never have foreseen.

The issue seemed straightforward: a blanket ban on pets within my strata scheme (apartment block), The Horizon Apartments. But beneath the surface lay a labyrinth of complexities and injustices waiting to be unravelled. When I first moved into The Horizon, I knew pets were coexisting within the community; multiple dogs and a cat, to be precise, were living on my floor alone. And yet, a draconian by-law dictated otherwise, condemning beloved companions to exile or clandestine transport in bags and shopping trolleys. It was a blatant disregard for property rights and the family bond between humans and their furry family members, a decree that relegated pet owners to the status of disobedient children.

I remember, after weeks of silence and avoidance, when I finally met with the chairman and secretary of our committee, they admitted they knew pets resided in the building and yet instructed me to sneak my pet in or face the risk of being a target. I was in disbelief that this was how grown adults allowed themselves to be treated in their homes. I responded by stating that I was not a teenager sneaking my boyfriend in through the window and would be putting forward a motion as it was within my legal rights.

My quest for change extended beyond convenience; it was a matter of right and wrong, a reflection of community standards, and a defence of property rights. Enforcing a blanket ban on pets was not just about controlling animals; it was a means of controlling their owners, curtailing their freedoms, and undermining their autonomy. Home has always held deep meaning, and a safe home is vital.

Neighbours given the power to regulate neighbours always shocked me; this was lazy legislation and required an understanding of the human dynamic. All I could think about were the many unique situations where this ludicrous accepted norm would create havoc - the barriers, the plight of those trapped in abusive relationships, and well-known limited housing options due to an unregulated "rule" seeking refuge. Barriers affected those needing companionship and those generally limited by housing options, including guide dog puppies in training who could go anywhere yet still required to be allowed into certain buildings. It was just unacceptable to me on so many levels.

However, as I dared to challenge the stagnant waters of the status quo, I was plunged into a storm of hostility and hypocrisy. Residents who shamelessly flouted the very by-laws they fervently defended hurled insults and condemnation at me. My motion, aimed at rectifying glaring inconsistencies, was met with obstructiveness from our Strata Manager and venomous resistance from those entrenched in their narrow-minded ways. The defining moment, the crystallisation of the emotional ineptitude I was up against, occurred as I made my way towards the back gate. A seemingly courteous man held the gate ajar for me, which I acknowledged with a simple "thank you." Yet, as we traversed beyond the confines of the property, his demeanour shifted abruptly. In a tone dripping with condescension, he demanded to know if I was the audacious individual attempting to disrupt the "fabric" of our community.

Although I articulated my intentions with measured composure, his impatience swelled into a rage as he aggressively interrogated me about challenging the pet policy. In a bold display of prejudice, he peered into my eyes and uttered words that reverberated like thunder on a clear day: "We've rid ourselves of millionaires in this building. You stupid little brown girl, you'll be gone in a week."

The shock rippled through me, tingling with disbelief. Did he indeed just reduce me to nothing more than a "stupid little brown girl"? Am I being racially abused for asking to rectify a situation that was set in the Dark Ages?

As I walked away, trembling with anger and resolve, I realised that this so-called community desperately needed a cultural metamorphosis and some lessons on leadership. I refused to stand idly by as a mere bystander in this struggle for justice and equity in our own homes of all places. The irony at this moment was that my dog, Angus, had not yet stepped foot into the building; I was the only person attempting to go about things in a manner of any maturity.

To the outside, it appeared this was a simple dispute about a cute dog, and of course, I would fight for my family member with all my heart - and Angus was undoubtedly an adorable dog. He was also the reason I had unearthed deep and entrenched systemic barriers and racism in our strata homes. I do not tolerate abuse of power and disrespect because it connects to bullying, which in many cases leads to violence. I knew the pattern of behaviour all too well.

The first year I challenged this medieval bylaw, I had little support. One neighbour stood by me as a shield from the very first moment, and then a few more came along. The majority either joined in on the abuse or stayed silent. Once again, the "bystanders" just glared at me. The disappointment still hits me; it's not one I think I will ever accept.

The general meetings in our scheme were marred by exceptional abuse towards me, with only a minority in attendance. At the same time, the majority were apathetic, a situation unlike anything I had experienced, and I worked in the construction industry, so that says something. I confided in my husband that if they were to take legal action based on egregiously false claims of breaching a bylaw arbitrarily enforced and, in my opinion, contrary to our property rights, I would vigorously defend myself. Unfortunately, they pursued precisely that course. Their arrogance bolstered their unwarranted confidence and irrational rage, clouding their judgment. The ensuing battle consumed me entirely, leading to a pause in my career as I found it impossible to juggle both responsibilities.

A minority of owners voted to commence proceedings in the NSW Civil and Administrative Tribunal (NCAT) against me, led by the strata committee. I filed a crossclaim seeking orders that the by-law was invalid. I was successful in this case; however, our committee was predictable, and they filed an appeal against the decision. The appeal was successful, and orders were made that Angus be removed from the apartment.

Appeals are typically challenged on legal grounds, but this judgment was rife with personal criticism directed at me. I found it troubling that the decision seemed to lack ethical handling.

My journey took me from the corridors of power to the halls of justice, where I encountered formidable adversaries and daunting setbacks. Legal proceedings ensued, each twist and turn adding layers of complexity to an already arduous battle. But with each setback, my resolve only strengthened, fuelled by a sense of purpose greater than myself. It was clear I was stepping on some toes that were benefiting from the total chaos within Strata walls, impacting millions within the place meant to reflect safety and sanctuary. How could we perform and contribute to the high levels that society places on us when our homes are a battleground?

Once the media got hold of the story, community support grew - so did the stream of messages, emails and mail I received. I struggled to keep up with them. The horror stories of bullying and abuse were rife and went well beyond pets. It seemed that strata owners had nowhere to turn. It was clear that politicians were not interested in a solution, that the police would not deal with the physical and verbal abuse I was subjected to, and that something was very wrong. Strata owners were falling through the cracks.

Though I wasn't easily intimidated, my opposition indeed attempted. They mobilised, and the gossip and abuse only intensified. Their behaviour resembled schoolyard bullies, yet they were adults, desperately trying to assert their superiority without realising how embarrassing and unintelligent their actions appeared. They accused me of being cunning, suggesting I aimed to increase property values by allowing pets and then selling, leaving others to deal with what they deemed a 43-level zoo.

One moment, they claimed someone was bankrolling my legal fees because I couldn't possibly afford them; the next, they accused me of having too much time and money, bored and labelling me as low-class. I was even labelled vexatious; these are just a few examples of the rumours that were circulating about me. What was more disturbing was that complete strangers bought into this mob mentality. People with certain profiles, strangers I had never conversed with, displayed immense disgust, and hate towards me due to childish gossip. Did these people not have minds of their own? Did they not question anything? How did they function in life outside The Horizon? It was disturbing and highly uncomfortable.

My challenge was never to react. Ironically, I found myself fighting for justice and advocating for the rights of pets. These creatures only bestowed unconditional love and never behaved as reprehensibly as some of these people did.

With politicians and governments refusing to intervene and the obstacles of a pandemic intensifying, I organised the very first e-petition for NSW. Until this point, it was paper-based. Without an official PR campaign, we gained over 17,184 signatures of the 20,000 required.

I also successfully organised an amendment in parliament, only to have it kicked down the hall for months. Luckily, I would not need to rely on either of these avenues. After two hearings, success in the first, overturned on appeal, I had 28 days to decide if I would take the risk and challenge their appeal at the highest court in our state. NSW Supreme Court of Appeal.

I did. I had to believe in justice, and the outcome I was working so hard towards was giving owners back their power in one of their most significant assets: their homes. Life was strained everywhere; the pandemic was taking its toll on many, and for me, this case represented safety, more housing options for women fleeing abusive relationships, giving back owners their power in their homes, and, of course, the right to pet ownership and companions that to many bring peace and unconditional love; and ultimately the essence and truest meaning of HOME.

October 12, 2020, justice triumphed. The Supreme Court of Appeal delivered a unanimous verdict in my favour, a landmark case, denouncing blanket bans on pets' by-laws as "harsh, unconscionable, or oppressive." A ruling that now placed restraints on the broad power overlooked given to Strata Committees, I achieved a judgment that went far beyond pets, our right to determine how we live in our apartments regardless of voting numbers.

It marked a watershed moment, a glorious victory for fairness, equity, and humanity, an enduring testament to the indomitable spirit of perseverance in the face of adversity. Yet, amidst the jubilation, I felt an overwhelming sense of exhaustion, the toll of the battle weighing heavily upon me. However, even in the glow of victory, the struggle persists.

The wounds of relentless harassment and bullying linger, a sad reminder of the sacrifices made in the pursuit of justice. Undeterred, I continued to lobby tirelessly, leaving nothing to chance. I ensured that parliament enacted my judgment in legislation, and they did ten months after my judgment was handed down.

What unfolded next was a rather ludicrous spectacle, a futile attempt to rewrite history and belittle the magnitude of my contributions. Those who once turned a cold shoulder to my cause now shamelessly sought to ride the coattails of its success, appropriating my triumphs for their selfish gains. My local MP, a vehement adversary in my battle, shamelessly paraded my victory as if it were his crowning achievement. Lawyers and academics who had idly stood by as mere spectators suddenly clamoured to hitch their wagons to my cause, eager to bolster their reputations.

Where were these individuals when I fought a battle no private citizen should ever have to shoulder? This task should have squarely fallen on the shoulders of our duly elected officials. Yet, there I stood, financing and fighting alone. Where were they as I sacrificed my health, career, and sanity, leading these legal battles without the backing and support that those in power could have easily provided? They, too, were bystanders, lurking in the shadows, waiting for the opportune moment to emerge and fully exploit the work I had yet to process and recover from.

These individuals would go on to give interviews about my case and push me aside as if they had funded and felt the battle scars of the six and a half years I spent changing laws and legislation. I couldn't help but wonder if I were a man or a white woman, would this have been the case?

I spent the following years guiding others through the labyrinth of new laws and regulations I had helped shape. This consuming passion led me to establish The Good Warrior - an initiative dedicated to educating, inspiring, and transforming bystanders into Warriors of Change. Our mission is to empower individuals and organisations to sincerely believe in the power of their voices to effect CHANGE, make an IMPACT, and leave a LEGACY that authentically mirrors their principles. Through workshops, storytelling, and keynote addresses, we strive to change culture and challenge laws and reforms that no longer serve us, creating leaders with courage and conviction.

The repercussions of my case are far-reaching, and the lessons learned continue to resonate. As entrepreneurs, we possess the courage and resilience to address issues our governments need to catch up on.

As leaders, we must lead by example, walking our talk and embracing challenges with unwavering resolve. Our purpose is a guiding force in how we live our lives. Though this experience challenged me, it also propelled me toward growth and transformation. If my journey can inspire a new generation of change-makers, innovators and advocates, the road ahead will be smoother for those who follow, and I will have fulfilled my purpose.

JO COOPER

Warrior for Change

https://esys.io/s/jo-cooper

Sophie Firmager
Entrepreneur & Author

ABOUT THE AUTHOR: SOPHIE FIRMAGER

Sophie Firmager is a visionary and idealist who has navigated life with a steadfast belief in the inherent goodness of people and that dreams, no matter how big, are within reach, even amidst challenges. Her journey from a determined young girl with a clear vision to a respected HR leader and entrepreneur stands as a testament to resilience, authenticity, and the transformative power of embracing one's true self.

With a foundation in psychology, Sophie forged a successful career in HR, driven by her ambition to become a young executive leader in a global iconic brand. Her tenure at Tiffany & Co. not only realized this aspiration but also revolutionized HR into a more heart-centered practice.

Through navigating adversities, Sophie learnt to get comfortable with discomfort in service of personal growth and evolution; cultivating self-love, embracing continuous learning, and unlocking mastery in mindset and emotional regulation and EQ - skills that became her superpowers and facilitated her dream life.

Sophie developed an uncanny ability to realize any goal she set herself through unconditional self-belief, embracing personal development, and surrounding herself with like-minded mentors and friends who believed in her and offered developmental feedback.

As she kicked her career goals, Sophie's values and definition of success shifted from corporate ambition to prioritizing parenting and contributing meaningfully to human flourishing. This personal evolution culminated in her venture into entrepreneurship in 2022, when she founded Realised Potential Group (RPG). RPG collaborates with leaders and organizations to unlock their potential through self-discovery, emotional intelligence, authenticity, and purpose-driven leadership.

Sophie is renowned for her expertise in executive coaching, strategic HR management, culture and leadership development, talent acquisition and branding, change management, and performance enablement. Her clients span Luxury Consumer Goods, Retail, Technology, Film, Entertainment, Not-For-Profit and Finance sectors, benefiting from her human-centric strategies and innovative programs.

Academically, Sophie holds tertiary qualifications in Psychology, NLP, Coaching and an Executive MBA. Her journey underscores a deep understanding that true success transcends corporate achievements—it lies in living authentically, embracing vulnerability, and making a positive impact.

Sophie's mission is clear: to enable individuals and organizations to cultivate authenticity, emotional intelligence, and purposeful leadership. Through personalized coaching, organizational workshops, podcasts, and RPG community networking events, she is dedicated to empowering others to unlock their full potential, live in accordance with their values and use their strengths to achieve their versions of success; shaping a world where success is defined by genuine connections, impactful actions, and living as the highest expressions of self.

CHAPTER 8

THE MAKINGS OF A DIAMOND: A JOURNEY OF SELF-DISCOVERY AND ACTUALIZATION

By Sophie Firmager

Have you ever felt a song resonate so deeply within you that it seemed to encapsulate your entire essence? For me, that song is "Diamonds" by Rihanna. Its rhythm and empowering lyrics embrace beauty, aesthetics, love, passion, strength, resilience, inner potential, self-actualization, and living life to its fullest — passions and strengths that have guided me to my career as an executive HR leader in luxury retail to becoming an entrepreneur.

When I see myself and those around me, I see beauty in the same way that I do when I gaze at a beautiful diamond. Beauty and love, to me, are the essence of who we are, our actions, and the world around us; beauty transcends superficial appearances and societal standards. Diamonds are formed under pressure, and what I've come to learn is that my journey into self-actualization was the culmination of many lessons, including the importance of getting comfortable with pressure and discomfort.

As a coach, I see qualities and abilities in my clients that they haven't yet uncovered within themselves. I help them discover their gifts, latent talents, and help them learn to trust their inner wisdom and intuition to become unstoppable in the face of challenges and in service of their goals. Beyond individual coaching, my work extends to helping teams and organizations identify their essence, purpose, values, and strengths to elevate their positioning, client experience, loyalty, and profitability.

How did I get here? They say that through trauma, you uncover your purpose, and life lessons become your greatest strengths and gifts to the world. I've faced my own struggles — living with self-doubt, low self-esteem masked as perfectionism, and an unyielding drive to prove my worth. Uncovering the secrets to self-discovery and self-actualization became my mission, and now I'm passionate about helping others accelerate their own path to self-love and actualization.

My chapter is a love letter to those navigating similar hurdles, unclear about their inner essence beneath layers of social conditioning. As we embark on this journey together, I invite you to reconnect with your own essence — to recognize its power, embrace its beauty, and unlock its limitless potential. Let us ignite the flame within and embark on a journey of self-discovery, empowerment, and transformation.

Childhood in Russia

> "There lived a certain man in Russia long ago. He was big and strong, in his eyes a flaming glow."
>
> — **Rasputin by Boney M**

Growing up in Communist Russia, I found myself navigating a landscape of contradictions – a mix of crazy, a blend of joy and happiness of family life and childhood.

I was born in 1983, a time when Russia was firmly entrenched in the policies of the Soviet Union under the leadership of Yuri Andropov. The political landscape was marked by stability, yet underlying tensions simmered beneath the surface.

Amidst this backdrop, my family life flourished. Drawn by the thrill of climbing trees and exploring nature, I found solace and joy in the simplicity of childhood. It was within the sanctuary of our home that I discovered a love of self-expression, eagerly embracing poetry, singing, dancing, and musical performances at our cherished family gatherings. In those moments, surrounded by love and laughter, I felt truly alive.

By the early 1990s, the winds of change swept across Russia as the Soviet Union dissolved, giving rise to an era of uncertainty and upheaval. It was during this tumultuous time that I first encountered the harsh realities of anti-Semitism and violence in our hometown of Pyatigorsk. Antisemitism itself wasn't new in Russia or to my family. My parents and the generations before them had to hide their religious identity through school and university as it was commonly known that Jewish students weren't accepted in mainstream settings and were ostracised at every opportunity.

In 1992, as unrest escalated, my parents made the courageous decision to uproot our lives and seek refuge in a foreign land. They left behind their comfortable jobs and sold everything we owned, determined to protect their children from the horrors unfolding in our hometown. With no other options in sight, we embarked on a journey to Australia. My parents didn't know the English language or have jobs waiting for them; all they had was hope for a better life for their children. They valued family beyond anything else and they believed in "better"; these became my foundational values and beliefs.

I always say that when you align your strengths with your purpose and values, you become unstoppable. In a journey fraught with danger and uncertainty, their values and purpose became their true north. Fleeing Russia at a time when many others were doing the same meant facing threats from gangs who preyed on desperate families like ours. Unable to wire money to Australia, we sewed our entire life savings into pillowcases and clothing, hoping to escape with our lives intact.

As we stood on the tarmac, preparing to board the plane to Australia, we were confronted by members of a criminal gang – who threatened us with violence if we did not hand over our money. In a heart-wrenching moment that will forever be indented in my memories, one of the gangsters pointed a gun to my little sister's head, threatening to shoot if we didn't give up all our life savings.

Though we made it out of Russia physically well, our arrival in Australia marked the beginning of a new chapter filled with hardship and struggle, putting my parents' mental health to the test. Without a dollar to our name, we were forced to live in government housing, struggling to make ends meet. Yet, amidst the adversity, my parents remained steadfast in their determination to provide a better future for me and my sisters. Their resilience and sacrifice served as the catalyst for my own relentless pursuit of success. In a land where our fortunes were reset to zero, I pledged to honor my parents' sacrifices by ascending to the heights of achievement, driven by an insatiable hunger to make them proud. However, as you'll come to learn, this pursuit of greatness came at a cost.

Migration to Australia

"Headin' for the islands. We're ready man and packed to go."

— **Gotta Go Home by Boney M**

Touching down in Sydney felt like a pilgrimage to a familiar yet new land. The warm January climate and sandy beaches gave me a strong sense of déjà vu. However, the transition wasn't smooth sailing; it was more like navigating a maze blindfolded while juggling flaming torches. Yet, this marked the beginning of my grand adventure into the mysteries of my inner and outer worlds.

Picture me, fresh off the plane, facing the daunting task of fitting in at school. As a chatterbox with a passion for self-expression but no knowledge of English, making friends was as daunting as teaching calculus to a goldfish. For a kid who thrived on human connection, this challenge hit harder than a ton of bricks.

But every cloud has a silver lining. In my case, that silver lining became a burning desire to master English faster than you could say, "g'day mate." School introduced challenges—loneliness, bullying—due to my linguistic shortcomings. However, these tough times nurtured my personal growth. Experiencing prejudice fuelled my passion for standing up for underdogs and minorities. These childhood experiences pushed me to learn, adapt, and discover new ways to express myself, through poetry, storytelling, and journaling —a rebellion against the tyranny of language barriers. Rebellion soon became my middle name as I entered my teens.

The Dawn of the Rebellious Era

> *"Here's to the crazy ones. The misfits. The rebels. The troublemakers…"*
>
> **— Steve Jobs**

Ah, the infamous teenage years—a time when hormones run wild and parents fear for their sanity. My poor parents were in for a wild ride when I entered the scene. Having raised a picture-perfect older sister, they were unprepared for my unique brand of teenage rebellion.

Blame it on stubbornness, a lack of earlier connection, or my innate desire to shake things up, but I saw the world differently to my parents. While they preferred to keep us on a tight leash, perhaps a remnant of our Russian past, I yearned for freedom like a caged bird.

Constant reminders of my mathematical ineptitude didn't help matters. Who wouldn't want to escape a house where every math problem felt like a personal failure? All I craved was freedom to explore my evolving sense of self, mingling with a new group of friends always up to something.

At 14, I ventured into the workforce. I wanted to help my parents but also carve out a life on my terms, free from external influences. Thus began my journey into self-discovery and actualization.

Adolescence—a time of rebellion, self-discovery, and questionable decisions. My teenage desire to belong led me into a relationship with the quintessential bad boy—a walking cliché from a Hollywood script. Smoking, mischief—he did it all. Caught between rebellion and affection, I found myself in real-life drama.

My parents weren't thrilled with my romance. "You don't need to date a troublemaker to learn it's a bad idea!" my mum argued, missing the allure of experiential learning. Her attempts to shield me from life's lessons only pushed me deeper into this romance.

In a move any teen would approve of, I ran away with my bad boy beau. Picture me, three garbage bags stuffed with belongings, sneaking into his car at 3am—the epitome of teenage rebellion. Yet, my grand escape didn't go as planned, and soon I was back home, nursing black eyes courtesy of my furious father.

But as I've learned, rainbows follow storms. Thanks to my aunt from Belgium, I found myself whisked away, into the land of chocolates and waffles. Belgium became my sanctuary, where I spread my wings and embraced youthful freedom.

Months later, back home, I faced university with wanderlust, enrolling into a Psychology degree, surprise, surprise! Amidst the chaos of my early 20s, love found me in Damon Firmager, my first true love and anchor through young adulthood. With a heart full of hope and dreams, I embarked on the next chapter of my wild and wonderful life.

Connection of Hearts

> *"You should let me love you. Let me be the one to, give you everything you want and need"*
>
> **— Let me love you by Mario**

Damon – a breath of fresh air in a world of recycled pick-up lines and superficial connections. From the moment we met, it was clear he was different – genuinely interested in the person behind the facade, captivated by the quirks and complexities that define me. What set Damon apart wasn't just his genuine interest; it was his unwavering belief in my potential and his commitment to seeing me thrive. Just as Mario intended, his love helped me learn to love myself.

Navigating the same party scene, dancing to the same beat, we crossed paths at a pivotal moment in our lives – ready to shed the shackles of our past and embrace a future filled with growth and possibility. Damon was a kindred spirit, equally self-expressive, a fellow seeker of truth and meaning in a chaotic world. We shared a passion for film and music, wrestled with emotional challenges, and believed in the power of self-development. Together, we embarked on a transformative journey, supporting each other every step of the way.

Hand in hand, we created the life of our dreams. Damon embraced my worldview of being drivers in our lives, not passengers, capable of achieving greatness through life's lessons. His awe for my philosophies matched my admiration for his presence in my life. Together, true, unconditional love unlocked our potential and turned dreams into reality. On our own, we were powerful; together, we were unstoppable.

Masculine Career Trajectory

"It's been a hard day's night, And I've been working like a dog."

— The Beatles

The relentless pursuit of a better life and financial success, ingrained in me since my family migrated to Australia, as well as a passion for people and human potential, fuelled my career in HR. Initially drawn into recruitment and later landing an in-house HR role, I had a quick succession into HR Management.

In 2009, I moved to a footwear retailer and expanded my expertise amid the company's accelerated growth. Delving deep into retail, I aligned people with the company's values and introduced a wellbeing program, reshaping HR to be more human-centric. Pursuing an MBA, I prepared for executive leadership, yet faced challenges breaking into the male-dominated executive team. Despite my achievements to date, I felt I needed to shed my feminine traits to be taken seriously, pushing myself to over-index on masculine qualities.

This shift strained my authenticity and ability to connect emotionally with my team, hindering trust and impacting my performance.

This brought back the low self-esteem and social anxiety I picked up as an 8-year-old girl navigating a new country and language. It all came to a head in a traumatic incident when I was giving a weekly HR Management update to the Head Office team, whilst heavily pregnant.

With the combination of anxiety and my unborn bundle of joy pressing heavily on my diaphragm, I became breathless, started to stutter, unable to get the words out, hyperventilating in front of a team I so yearned the respect of. After what seemed like hours, but lasted a few minutes, I eventually stepped out of the spotlight, desperately wanting to crawl under a rug and never show my face again.

This became a lesson on the power of our thoughts. The internal rhetoric that I was a terrible leader became a self-fulfilling prophecy. Through this, I learnt to use my thoughts and beliefs more wisely. Instead of letting this traumatic incident and fear keep me from speaking again, I leaned into the discomfort, just as life forced me to as a child 20 years earlier, and enrolled myself into Toastmasters, a community public speaking program, and through repetition, regained my confidence and love for speaking.

I kept at it because, as a kid, I loved all forms of verbal expression, whether it be speaking, acting, dancing or singing in front of audiences. This lesson of becoming comfortable with discomfort, which started for me as a child navigating a new country and finding school difficult, became one of my most crucial superpowers to date. Later, I became more intentional about it, knowing that every difficulty was essential for my evolution, whether it be the pressure of a deadline or throwing myself into the unchartered territory of a new business requiring skills I didn't have, such as sales and marketing, I knew that I could thrive in discomfort and have subsequently learnt to enjoy high pressured environments.

Pregnancy and parental leave offered a transformative pause, refocusing my priorities on family and rediscovering my femininity. During this period, a pivotal leadership event introduced me to Martin Seligman's *Positive Psychology*, sparking a profound shift in my approach to life and career.

My trajectory to this point was defined by ambition, resilience, and the pursuit of excellence in a challenging environment. Through successes and setbacks, I learned the importance of balance, self-reflection, and embracing authenticity to achieve meaningful impact.

Enlightenment - From Thought to Reality

> *"Wisest is she who knows she does not know."*
>
> **— Socrates**

My journey into enlightenment began with Jostein Gaarder's "Sophie's World" during my teenage years. This book delved into the history of humanity, drawing wisdom from numerous philosophers and scholars, with Socrates emerging as my greatest influence. His quote, "Wisest is she who knows she does not know," initially struck me as a call for humility and lifelong learning. However, it took me twelve years to truly embody its profound meaning. Early in my career, I faced harsh criticism for my mistakes, which instilled in me a deep fear and anxiety about admitting shortcomings. It wasn't until my early thirties that I began to shed these fears, actively seeking and embracing feedback on both my flaws and strengths. This shift allowed me to engage in self-reflection and focus on progress rather than perfection.

Immersed in books, documentaries, and personal explorations of Positive Psychology, Quantum Physics, and Epigenetics, I started to grasp the interconnectedness of mind, body, and spirit. Embracing the understanding that I am the architect of my reality, capable of manifesting my deepest aspirations, liberated and empowered me.

However, my greatest influence was my son Zac, who transformed every fibre of my being. Feeling him grow within me was a marvel, a poignant reminder of our bodies' miraculous ability to nurture life. The moment I held Zac in my arms for the first time, I was overwhelmed by his beauty and the profound miracle of his existence. It was then that I silently vowed to give him the best possible start in life. It was also from this point in my life that I began to see every human walking this earth as somebody's precious child.

From the instant I became pregnant, my body became sacred ground. I treated it with reverence, honouring its role in safeguarding and nurturing the precious life growing within. Zac's presence awakened a deep love and respect for my body, dispelling years of self-criticism and negative body image. Embracing motherhood, my feminine energy flowed naturally, awakening empathy, intuitive wisdom, and boundless creativity.

This transformation came as I released the need for certainty and control that had dominated my corporate life. In the workplace, where certainty and efficiency reign supreme, every detail is meticulously planned. Parenting, however, thrust me into uncertainty, akin to navigating an ocean without a map. In this beautiful chaos, I found mindfulness and a deep appreciation for life's unpredictability. Zac taught me the joy of simply being, shifting my focus from relentless achievement to embracing the present moment.

Just as diamonds are created under pressure, human beings reach self-actualization through adversity. My troubles at work and my struggle with parenting led to an evolved, wiser and more resilient me. Shortly after Zac's birth, I found myself quite literally drawn into the world of diamonds as HR Director for Tiffany & Co. in Australia and New Zealand. This opportunity seamlessly aligned with my journey, marking a new chapter where I could integrate my newfound wisdom and experience into my career.

Part 7: Realized Potential

"We start believing now that we can be who we are"

— Grease by Frankie Valli

My experience at Tiffany was nothing short of amazing. It wasn't just about the jewellery; it was about the people, the people-first culture, and the opportunities for travel that truly resonated with me. Initially drawn to contribute at a higher level in a global firm, I discovered much more—a deep understanding of human psychology and a newfound appreciation for aesthetics that awakened a side of me I never knew existed.

When people learned of my role at Tiffany, it seemed to click for them. They would say, "Of course. Tiffany suits you perfectly, and you suit Tiffany." What they meant was that Tiffany embodied style, luxury, and a femininity beyond imagination—qualities they saw in me before I fully recognized them in myself. They say the body doesn't lie; you cannot deny your true nature—it will always find a way to shine through.

I had always cherished beauty and excellence, and at Tiffany, I found both in abundance. I made it my mission to deepen the personal connection within the team, fostering human bonds among colleagues and clients alike. Drawing from positive psychology, I helped leaders embody their truest selves, unlocking their potential and inspiring their teams to do the same. Authenticity and mindfulness enabled meaningful connections—a camaraderie that fuelled collaboration, a flow of creativity, and optimal performance. With clients, these connections fostered openness, trust, and bespoke service, creating memorable experiences and lasting loyalty.

Every experience in life is a lesson, and Tiffany provided ample learning opportunities. I mastered the intricacies of a highly matrixed organization, delved into workforce planning, organizational design, and budgeting, and embraced global collaboration on transformative projects. Yet, as I neared the end of my tenure, I felt a growing desire to focus on my strengths rather than spread myself thin across the breadth of HR.

I realized I was leaning too heavily into masculine qualities again — pushing myself relentlessly, working excessive hours, and losing sight of my aspiration to be a present parent to Zac. Stepping away, I embarked on a new journey with my own leadership development firm, a bold move beyond my comfort zone. Embracing uncertainty, I thrived under pressure, learning and adapting swiftly.

Choosing creative freedom, feminine energy, and love as guiding principles, I aligned my business with my evolved values. Empowered by authenticity, mindfulness, and emotional intelligence, I dedicated myself to helping leaders create human-centric, prosperous organizations and helping individuals unlock their potential by aligning with their values, purpose, and strengths.

Each step in my entrepreneurial journey, each challenge conquered and triumph celebrated, fortified my resilience and deepened my passion for living authentically. Today, I stand as a testament to the transformative power of embracing femininity, self-love, and personal empowerment.

Conclusion: Unlocking My Essence

In concluding this chapter of my hero's journey, I realize I've been chasing an illusion, perpetuating a cycle of unfulfillment inherited from my parents' struggles as immigrants. The pursuit of a "better life" obscured the true richness already present. This revelation struck me profoundly. I found my way back to my inner child, infused with the wisdom of adulthood.

In my relentless quest, I had overlooked genuine joy, creative freedom, and abundance that I have always had access to in spite of my status and level of achievements. Venturing into entrepreneurship enabled me to rediscover love for myself beyond societal roles. Tears of recognition washed away long-held traumas, freeing me. I understood that I possessed all I needed within and around me to flourish—skills, a loving family, supportive friends, a cherished clientele, a fulfilling career, a beautiful home, and enriching experiences.

At forty, I stand at the cusp of a new beginning, embracing my best decade with faith in life's abundance and my aligned purpose. I've learned to embrace my femininity, lean into discomfort, and trust life's flow. My journey, ongoing like yours, has led me to living my truth, inspiring others to do the same. Grateful for every experience shaping me, I eagerly anticipate what I'll manifest next.

SOPHIE FIRMAGER

Entrepreneur & Author

https://esys.io/s/sophie-firmager

Cristina Santangelo
Inclusive Image Consultant & Style Coach

ABOUT THE AUTHOR: CRISTINA SANTANGELO

Meet Cristina Santangelo, a passionate and experienced Certified Image Consultant and Style Coach dedicated to elevating individuals' personal and professional brand image. Originally from the beautiful city of Rome, Cristina brings with her over two decades of corporate finance experience from Italy and Australia.

Her love for power dynamics and non-verbal expressions of power through visual aesthetics and body language led her to a pivotal career change a few years ago. With her Italian heritage, Cristina has always had a keen eye for beauty in all its forms. She believes that what you wear communicates who you are and dictates how others perceive and treat you.

Her mission is to empower individuals to amplify their 'visual voice' and boost their confidence through the power of clothing, colour, and personal style. Cristina is passionate about changing the way individuals view themselves in the mirror. She wants the mirror to be a source of empowerment rather than frustration, aiming to bring a smile to your face.

When she's not transforming lives through her work, Cristina loves spending time with her husband and two teenagers. Although they've mastered the ancient teenage art of dodging spending time with their parents, Cristina cherishes every moment she spends with her family.

CHAPTER 9

BEAUTY IN THE WORLD OF PRETTINESS

The media bombards us every day with images of women who supposedly embody the true meaning of beauty. It usually involves being very young, super slim, long-haired, and, these days, having a waist the size of a wasp and a backside you could park a tea tray on.

Society and fashion fads have created a very narrow definition of beauty, and unfortunately, it changes with every new fashion trend. Twiggy was the "It" girl of the 60s, but being built like an ironing board, no one would give her a second glance today unless she had a Brazilian butt lift, a boob job, and fillers that make her lips look like bratwurst. And let's not forget the hair. Hers was short and absolutely wouldn't do. To be considered beautiful today, your hair must be long, straight, and have a middle parting.

Honestly, trying to keep up with beauty trends is exhausting.

As a teenager, I conformed to the stereotypical Barbie type. I even remember my teacher once calling me a stereotypical white girl - and it wasn't a compliment! I was the epitome of privilege - a pretty girl who effortlessly won the genetic lottery and fit perfectly into society's narrow definition of beauty - tall, slender, with milky white skin, and blonde (between you and me, I'm a bottle blonde, but don't tell anyone). It's a stereotype that was tailor-made for girls who looked like me, and I've unwittingly reaped its rewards. Most people don't realise that the downside is that people assume that girls are either endowed with good looks or brain cells.

People thought my looks meant that my life was perfect and that I had the world at my feet. They didn't realise that they made me feel frustrated and inadequate because I wanted to be worth so much more than what I looked like. I wanted a meaningful purpose and for people to see me as much more than my appearance. I wanted to be seen as and feel like a woman with substance.

I want to challenge the superficial mindset of beauty. Have you ever really considered what beauty truly means to you, especially as a woman who has faced various life challenges such as divorce, pregnancies, miscarriages, menopause, and the barriers we encounter in our careers? Let's ignore the media hype and noise and truly reflect on this.

At the age of 47, I have switched careers twice and left a successful, well-paid corporate finance position to pursue a new path as a certified image consultant.

Every woman is inherently beautiful and deserves to care for herself and dress in a manner that showcases her beauty and evokes a sense of well-being.

MY TEENS

Growing up in a small seaside village near Rome, at the age of 15, I was cast for a television program, handpicked from a group of girls at a dance concert. This led me into the world of modelling, and I even made it to the final stages of Miss Italy. However, despite the fleeting fame, I didn't feel comfortable in the spotlight. I was just a teenager—quiet, shy, and reserved, and I felt out of place in the world of pageantry.

Standing in the spotlight felt overwhelming, as if I were on a stage without knowing my lines. Autograph requests left me feeling even more out of place – me? Really? My reserved nature clashed with the storm of attention, leaving me feeling like a fish out of water in the world of fame and glamour. I also yearned to be seen as having substance.

After high school, I was determined to pursue a university education, becoming the first in my family to do so. I felt a burning ambition, a drive to show that I was more than just a pretty face. I was proving to myself and others that I had the intellect, determination, and tenacity to succeed beyond superficial appearances.

University became my proving ground, where I imagined myself travelling for work and attending meetings in bustling cities around the world. These dreams really fuelled my ambition and guided my choices during that time. While my friends were partying, I diligently studied at home, immersed in my books.

Was all the hard work during university worth it? Graduating with top marks remains one of my proudest accomplishments to date. I still vividly recall the moment my professor addressed me as "Dottore," a title in Italy conferred to graduates across various disciplines. It is amazing how a single word, a title, can be so validating and gratifying. I can also tell you that it felt a million times better than "Barbie".

"The two most important days in your life are the day you are born and the day you find out your why"

- Mark Twain

Looking back, I wish someone had emphasised the importance of discovering my purpose. Despite doing well in my studies and sports, I never found something that truly inspired me. I didn't feel especially talented or passionate about anything specific. As a result, I often prioritised practical concerns like job prospects and financial stability over pursuing my true passion.

MY TWENTIES

After graduating with a finance and business studies degree, I landed my dream job in mergers and acquisitions, where I met my future husband, Andrea. I started travelling extensively for work, working very long hours and shuttling between Rome and Milan to meet clients. It was just as I had always envisioned—a career-driven, independent woman making her mark in the business world. I was very happy, but there was still something missing.

In 2002, Andrea and I went backpacking in Australia for a month, spending a week in Sydney. We were so naive and saw Australia as a dreamland, imagining kangaroos bounding joyfully around the CBD. We even tried to get job interviews with big Sydney banks!

We stayed in a hostel near Hyde Park, and every morning we got dressed up in fancy suits for our interviews. I'll never forget the curious glances from other backpackers, as if we were creatures from another planet masquerading as job-seeking professionals.

Landing a job in just one week proved to be a bit of a dream, but the experience was not in vain. We met many friendly people who were keen to help and gave us good advice. Sydney stole my heart with its beaches and infinite horizon. Then and there, I made a silent vow to return one day.

It took me a year to perfect my negotiation skills, but I finally convinced Andrea to leave his job and return to Sydney with me. In

2004, we finally embarked on the adventure that I always yearned for, trading our secure job and the ancient streets of Rome for the white beaches of Sydney. With little more than thirty pieces of luggage (all absolutely necessary for survival) and a sense of excitement, we arrived in a city where we were strangers, leaving behind family and friends who thought we were crazy. I'll never forget the sight of the hotel reception overflowing with our suitcases, containing our entire lives packed into just a few (maybe more than a few) bags.

Our initial plan was simple: find casual work to immerse ourselves in the local culture and improve our English before pursuing more professional opportunities. I tried my hand at various casual jobs, including a brief stint at a deli where my skills with a knife left much to be desired. Apparently, slicing my beloved prosciutto was not my forte. Andrea wasted no time diving into the world of pizza delivery, much to the dismay of my father, who couldn't accept the transition from "prestigious" corporate finance to prosciutto-slicing lady and pizza delivery boy.

In those early days, every dollar earned felt like a triumph, especially when generous customers left a $1 tip. We scrimped and saved wherever we could, opting to live in a modest studio in Elizabeth Bay instead of a more spacious one-bedroom apartment for a mere $25 saving. It wasn't a matter of affordability; instead, it was a conscious choice to embrace our new adventure.

After only a few weeks, my career in cold meat slicing was cut short when I landed my first contract in Corporate Banking, much to the joy and relief of my father. It makes me laugh to remember how, on that same day, Andrea asked me if he could quit his pizza delivery job. Oh, and the treat of having a luxury dinner at Woolloomooloo Wharf is still one of my most unforgettable meals.

Now, I have a confession to make about this new high-flying job. Whenever the phone rang, I resorted to a rather unorthodox strategy of pretending to have a sudden overwhelming need to visit the restroom (I'm sure my colleagues thought I had an incontinence problem). I just dreaded the possibility of a conversation with a caller with a solid Australian accent because I struggled to understand a word they were saying. So, instead of risking embarrassment, I bought myself time by listening to their voicemail multiple times until I could confidently discern the details. And even then, I insisted that callers email me their requests as 'per company policy', just to be sure. How stressful.

One fateful day, I found myself thrust into my first client meeting alongside my Director, only to be abruptly abandoned after a mere five minutes as he hurried off to another appointment. I was left alone and completely lost. How could he leave me like that? Believe me when I say that I couldn't understand anything the client said. I vividly recall the sheer horror I felt as I strolled back into the office, only to be greeted by my Director and asked about the client meeting. I blurted out the infamous line with every ounce of courage: "Oh, you know, he didn't really say anything important."

MY THIRTIES

My priorities and career goals shifted when my baby boy Luca was born in November 2007. Returning to work after maternity leave didn't feel right, and I realised that my priorities in life had shifted. Instead of returning to my old job, I started looking for new opportunities.

This time, the interview process felt awkward, and I wondered if I should disclose that working long hours and on weekends and travelling were no longer options. Unsure of how they would be received, I questioned whether to disclose these changes during interviews, especially in an era like the late noughties.

Despite the challenges, I managed to land a new job in the strategy team at Qantas (I was so excited about the flight benefits!). It was going well until, a year later, the global financial crisis hit, and I was laid off. Although it was initially upsetting, it was a hidden blessing as it gave me a chance to reflect on what I wanted. I realised I had lost interest in the corporate world, which was no longer where I wanted to be.

> **"Success is not final. Failure is not fatal.
> It's the courage to continue that counts"**
>
> *- Winston Churchil*

My beautiful daughter, Camilla, was conceived during my redundancy. It was then that I made the bold decision to venture into entrepreneurship and launched my first start-up—an Italian online store specialising in wedding favours called "mybomboniere"

Starting my own business was a significant transition for me, one that came with its own set of challenges. At first, I felt a sense of loss—loss of the status I had worked hard to achieve as a career woman to prove that I was so much more than just a Barbie doll. The stability of not having a predictable paycheck was also daunting. It felt like I had lost some of my independence, even though my husband was incredibly supportive.

However, the business flourished rapidly, keeping me busy managing suppliers, engaging customers, and handling imports. This period was marked by both triumphs and challenges as I navigated the unpredictable landscape of the online world.

MY FORTIES

In 2017, after seven years, I made the decision to sell my business and return to the corporate world as my children had grown older.

While part of the decision was due to the challenges of managing an online business in Italy from Australia, I also wanted to set an example for my children.

They had only ever seen me working from home and didn't fully understand the effort I was putting in. Perhaps, deep down, I also longed to regain the sense of security and recognition that comes with a stable income and a prestigious position. In many ways, it was a journey of self-validation—a quest to reaffirm my worth and capabilities, not just in the eyes of others, but for myself. I was still looking for validation of my worth from external sources. I also clearly had not found my purpose yet.

"There comes a time when you look into the mirror and you realise that what you see is all you'll ever be, and then you accept it or you kill yourself, or you stop looking in mirrors"

- Tennessee Williams

Finally, in my mid-forties, I discovered my passion and purpose to empower women to feel beautiful and confident. I realised that wearing the right clothes and colours that make you feel beautiful, taking care of your skin, and using makeup to enhance your natural beauty make a huge difference to a woman's confidence and energy. Often, we feel confused about our own identity – are we old or young, mother or wife, modern or classic, attractive or past our "prime" (what a load of nonsense that is!). This is where I step in and help my clients rediscover their mojo.

People have always seen me as someone driven, brave, and strong. But there have been so many times when I've had to stop and think about what I really want and how to get there. I've had to make tough decisions and face my fears. Sometimes, you just need to take a chance and trust that things will work out, so I left the corporate world once more and decided to follow what I now found I truly loved.

I started my journey to becoming a stylist by enrolling in a Colour Analysis course when I was in Rome after the COVID-19 pandemic to introduce more hues to my wardrobe and my life.

If you were a colour, which one would you be?

Understanding which colours suit us means reflecting on and identifying the shades that make us feel more confident, more beautiful, and happier. Our individual colour preferences can reveal a lot about our personality and attitude. While anyone can wear any colour, it is the specific shade, tone, tint, or intensity that determines if it complements our natural features.

Colour analysis is a technique that aims to discover which colour palette will enhance our natural beauty by analysing our skin tone, eyes, and hair. It's fascinating to note that Hollywood costume designers were the original image consultants, realising that colour could be used to enhance a character as cinema transitioned from black and white to Technicolor. If you watch old movies featuring screen legends like Grace Kelly, you can see how their stylists consistently stick to the same colour palette.

The four primary color palettes are named after the four seasons (Spring, Summer, Autumn, and Winter) because each palette draws inspiration from the colors found in nature during that time of year. Each season is further divided into three sub-seasons.

When choosing a color palette, it's important to consider three variables: your undertone (warm or cool, as lightness does not necessarily mean coolness), your intensity (bright or soft), and your value (light or dark). Your hair color, whether blonde or dark, does not matter. To determine your best color palette, I use a professional draping kit.

Then, there's a more psychological aspect of colour that I adore. Colour psychology is the science that helps us understand the language of colour and the profound impact it has on how we look, feel, and behave, as well as how others perceive us. Established research suggests that each colour - every tone and every tint - has a specific effect on us at an emotional, mental, and physical level.

Different colours trigger different feelings. Just think of how the colours in nature affect us: the yellow of the sun fills us with happiness and optimism, the greens of the forest give us the feeling of peace and tranquillity, and a dark-grey sky makes us want to stay in bed under the covers.

Would you like to know which colour palette corresponds to your personality?

Over 2,400 years ago, the Greek philosopher Hippocrates studied human behaviour and theorised that people can be identified as one of four temperaments. In modern times, it has been discovered that the four basic colour seasons (i.e., Winter, Summer, Autumn, and Spring) fit perfectly into Hippocrates' theory. Links between colour and personality can give real insight into who we are. Each colour group reflects a certain type of personality, and the corresponding colour palette can be used for your personal branding, fashion styling, and even home styling! If you are curious, please go to my website (www.cristinasantangelo.com) and take a 60-second quiz to discover your colour personality and your colour palette.

Rediscovering colour to put ourselves back in the spotlight.

As an image consultant, I help women recognise their strengths and weaknesses so they're not enslaved by external fashion trends or input. I help you choose what enhances you, not what the latest fashion fad tells you to wear. No one has the wrong body. You can wear anything, as long as you do it well.

Playing with colours, textures, and accessories that make us feel amazing is energising and something that everyone has the right to experience. Embracing your unique and most flattering colour palette and understanding how to complement your body with the best lengths, cuts, and shapes will bring your style, self-confidence, and personal brand to a whole new level. Your self-perception will elevate, and so will your energy, making it magnetic.

My mission is to inspire and empower women to intentionally elevate their personal styles as an act of self-love, no matter what size and age they are. Beauty is not something we should give up on as we age or because we think we're too tall, too short, too thin, too fat or anything else you can think of. I think beauty becomes a problem when we give it a name and a surname.

Fashion is a silent language, an extension of who we are.

How we dress can be a tool to communicate our message, reflect or mask how we feel. I would even go so far as to say that those clothes can make you feel confident. It's hard to feel insecure when you look your best.

Now, whilst society constantly bombards us with the latest beauty, plastic surgery, and beauty trends, all telling us how to look more "beautiful" (in whose opinion is what I would like to know), society also conditions us to think that taking care of how we look is vain and shallow. If you take pains to look your best because you respect and take pride in yourself, you're vain, and if you don't, you're ugly.

My advice – there are no rules. Just do what makes you feel alive and wear what you love.

How we dress wields a significant influence. Consider this experiment: put on your most beloved ensemble, complete with high heels, and venture out for a stroll or a grocery run. Then, switch to a black hoodie and flats, and repeat the outing. Did you sense a shift in your confidence? Did you observe any changes in how people reacted to you?

You might be laughing at this point and thinking, "Cristina, it's just a dress," but I'm sure you have one outfit that gives you a spark when you wear it. Remember, that is the spark you bring to the world.

We all lead busy lives and may think that focusing on our wardrobe is the last thing we need because we juggle kids, a stressful job, and never-ending bills.

How we present ourselves to the world can significantly impact various aspects of our lives. Whether it's improving our social life, finding a romantic partner, or securing a promotion, our wardrobe plays a significant role. It has the power to help us embody the person we aspire to be and expedite our journey towards that goal.

> **"The sidelines are not where you want to live your life. The world needs you in the arena!"**
>
> *- Tim Cook*

Dressing to look and feel your best is completely within your control and is a skill that can be learned. Once you do, getting dressed will be easy and enjoyable.

Are you ready to become an even more beautiful version 2.0 of yourself? Now is your time to shine!

CRISTINA SANTANGELO
Inclusive Image Consultant & Style Coach

https://esys.io/s/cristina-santangelo

Sue-Ann Wilson

Taking leaps of faith to define your authentic life: Sue-Ann Wilson's purpose.

ABOUT THE AUTHOR: SUE-ANN WILSON

Sue-Ann Wilson has embraced taking leaps of faith whilst on the journey to creating a life that is authentic to her and her family. Becoming a mother has fuelled a broader purpose, leading her to create initiatives that support and empower parents whilst balancing the tightrope of professional and personal lives. Sue-Ann's story demonstrates how our past experiences, no matter how difficult, can be transformed into powerful motivators for positive change. Her journey is a testament to the idea that joy can be found in embracing leaps of faith which can be daunting to fuel our passions and create meaningful impact whilst leading a life that is personally purposeful.

CHAPTER 10

THE PATH TO FINDING MYSELF: EMBRACING THE JOY IN TAKING A LEAP OF FAITH TO CREATE PIVOTAL MOMENTS IN LIFE

EMBRACING LEAPS OF FAITH

Have women been deceived for years? We have been led to believe that we can have and do everything—to have a successful career, run the seamless operation of a perfectly organised household and keep the spark in our relationships going. We have been told we can be high-performing business leaders, perfect partners and mothers. I believe the saying goes: *you can, but just not all at once.*

Many of us have worked hard to attain this ideal, only to fall short, blame ourselves for not being perfect, and be riddled with guilt. The reality is that we have been trying to achieve the impossible. Plus, as we get older and wiser in knowing what we want, we find that our priorities shift, and it may not even be what we actually want for our lives.

If you are a busy woman juggling the responsibilities of raising a family and pursuing a career, or if you are a working mom-to-be contemplating your future, and you are ready to redefine what a successful life looks like—one that is authentic to you and your family—I have written this chapter for you.

I embarked on the journey to discover my true vision when I realised that my children were moving on to the next phase of life. This meant I had to evolve as a parent to meet their needs. I had to dig deep and truly understand what I stood for and wanted in life. It was easy enough to continue on my career path, following the linear progression of promotional opportunities. Still, something was not sitting right with me anymore, and I felt there was more to unpack. As I embarked on this journey of exploration, I found it to be a complex and often confronting experience. However, until I addressed the issues within me, the sense of restlessness I felt stubbornly refused to go away.

My journey of self-discovery wasn't easy; I had to confront some uncomfortable truths. However, it was incredibly worthwhile because it allowed me to grow, understand myself better, and ultimately live a more authentic and fulfilling life. I was born in Kuala Lumpur, Malaysia, and grew up in a small town called Butterworth on an island called Penang. I have fond memories of time spent in the shophouse where we lived with my grandmother, who ran a little corner store next to my grandfather's barbershop. My parents' work brought us to Brunei and later Singapore, where my brother was born.

When I was 19, one of the leaps of faith I took was moving to Sydney. Growing up in Asia, I yearned to explore a new environment and expose myself to a new culture. I enrolled at the University of New South Wales and undertook a Bachelor of Science and Mathematics with a major in Psychology. I remember feeling the butterflies in my tummy as the plane took off from Singapore, signalling the start of my new adventure. University life allowed me to enjoy the freedom and independence I craved. I've always loved working with children, and after graduating, I worked in child protection services. It was the ultimate life lesson in not judging and applying empathy to situations foreign to me, having lived in Singapore.

On reflection, my career has been sewn together by taking a series of "leaps of faith" to broaden my expertise and try new industries. I moved from being a child protection caseworker working "in the field" to working in the corporate partnerships teams at a not-for-profit.

When the opportunity arose, I decided to try the legal industry. The transition to legal was challenging. Everything was vastly different from what I was used to. I gave it my all to get up to speed with tight deadlines and understand the intricacies and complexity of the subject matter. I started to enjoy working in law, and 15 years passed, during which I became a mother.

We welcomed our first son in 2014. We depended on each other to run the household. Daycare was notoriously expensive and difficult to get into, and knowing how long the waiting lists were was incredibly stressful. As my parental leave ended, I considered multiple daycare centres as part of the childcare arrangement.

In despair, I sought the advice of an ex-boss, to whom I will always be grateful, as she guided me through navigating motherhood and career ambition. Her advice was to have a foot in the workforce to stay relevant and find a childcare arrangement that would give me the peace of mind I needed. There was no skirting around the fact that it would be challenging, but the younger years were a stage of parenthood that would pass as the kids grew older and managing them got easier in some ways. I bit the bullet and invested in having a nanny who cared for my children like her family.

Knowing my son was in great hands, I kicked things up a notch at work. I identified a need and created a business case for a new program dedicated to enhancing client experiences, resulting in new revenue streams and stronger relationships with existing clients. During the endorsement process, a lack of confidence hit hard, and then hormones hit even harder when I discovered I was pregnant with my second son. My self-doubt was needless because I got the support to proceed with a pilot program, which gave me the energy to battle morning sickness. With a fantastic team and visionary partners at the firm, we delivered untapped business growth, which had a knock-on effect through advocacy and attracting new clients into the business!

My second son was born in 2017, and we settled into our new routine as a family of four. I enjoyed being a mother and loved spending time with the Wilson boys, as I called the trio (husband included), but the routine of having two young kids was often overwhelming. Sometimes, it felt like I was on an endless spin cycle where I spent all week working only to greet the weekend with sports commitments, grocery runs, loading and unloading the dishwasher for the umpteenth time, and endless cycles on the washing machine only to unpack what seemed like 100 little items of clothing, which were cute but time-consuming, especially when matching pairs of socks had to be found.

My husband and I tag-teamed to run the household: one of us would cook, and the other would put the kids in the bath or tidy up post-dinner. The other would put the kids to bed and, more often than not, crash out for the night, too. During particularly rough weeks when the kids were ill, I often asked my husband if there was another way to survive the next decade of parental duties. I was starting to feel the weight of the mental load.

A move back to Singapore at the end of 2019 presented an opportunity to switch things up. Given how much we loved Sydney, it wasn't an easy decision, and I felt I had somewhat gotten the hang of balancing family and career. We weighed that against being closer to my family and the travel and cultural experiences we could share. This time, we took a leap of faith as a family of four. I recall the anticipation of wondering what imprint this experience would have on us as the 40-foot container with all our possessions made its way out of our driveway to Singapore's shores.

COVID-19 impacted our start in Singapore, but I am grateful to have been able to be in the same country as my family. I reminded myself that we were together to weather out this unexpected event, and the constant search for necessities such as toilet paper was a minor inconvenience in the bigger scheme of things. Our family helped us through care packages and arrived with activities for the kids and practical necessities.

When COVID-19 restrictions eased, we got to experience life in Singapore, which included spending time with extended family and travelling, which I wanted us to experience as a family. As my kids became older and commitments grew during this pivotal stage of my life, I sometimes resisted change, which was very unlike me. "Old me" took leaps of faith to create the change in my life I wanted. I started to fear that "failure from taking a leap of faith to create change" would be too much to bear.

Given how our children's issues have evolved today, I knew I had to evolve as a parent and that I couldn't "rinse and repeat" parenting styles from previous years. By undertaking a journey of self-discovery to understand my vision for my family and my core values, I have learned that the truest form of success comes from aligning how we live with our core values.

While on my journey of exploration, I worked through the stages below to uncover my vision for myself and my family—think of it as a transformation compass.

SEEK CLARITY

Beyond seeking the purpose of our lives, one of the most impactful journeys we undertake is exploring our personalities and sense of self. Some people never find the answer to "Who am I?" while others discover it at a remarkably young age. Humanity has been on this quest for millennia. So, how can we uncover our true selves?

I've discovered that true success stems from exploring your inner self and genuinely listening to your thoughts. The key lies in self-reflection. Ask yourself, "How did I get here, and where am I now?" Identify your guiding principles by considering the values and beliefs that resonate most deeply. Delve into why you've chosen these principles to define your ideal life. These are just a few questions that can guide you in uncovering the answer to "Who am I?"

"Who am I?" to some is the more accessible part of the quest for who we are because we're accustomed to asking it. Both adolescence and adulthood involve a long-standing tradition of searching for identity. However, the second half of the search for our identity, "What do you stand for?" is far more challenging to answer, I've found. What do I advocate for? You must first believe that standing for something is essential before you can respond. Believing in something is not the same as standing for it. Beliefs may be private and personal, but standing up for something calls for action.

Standing up is silent yet visible. It was a powerful feeling to believe that I could stand for something. It's not just about existing or seeking my identity or happiness, but about choosing what I genuinely stand for. Beyond my existence, what can I do because I represent something greater than myself?

Knowing who you are and what you stand for is power.

ACKNOWLEDGE AND RELEASE YOUR FEARS

On my journey to understand myself, I discovered that I grapple with a fear of "getting it wrong" and how it might impact our family's future. But is it fear of getting it wrong, or is there an underlying shadow value of always needing to get it right? While some fear is essential to keep us safe, when it goes into overdrive, it creates unhelpful anxiety about future possibilities that may never happen.

I found that many of my anxieties were unfounded. Another common fear I discovered in myself was the fear of not being worthy enough. Do you experience this fear? I still feel it today, as I have my entire life. This often links back to the idea of women being able to do and have it all. What happens when we fail at this impossible quest? We think we're not good enough. The solution is acknowledging and addressing these fears with self-compassion and realism.

Regarding fears, the truth is that feeling afraid from time to time is normal. Fear keeps us on our toes and prevents us from making reckless decisions. The trick is not to let it become anxiety that stops you from pursuing your goals and living with regrets. Here are the lessons I've learned from my experience and seeking the advice of professionals.

The first crucial step is to recognise your fear. Fears are common, but they often remain hidden in the recesses of our minds, going unrecognised and unaddressed if we dismiss them.

What scares you? Write it down. Journalling not only brings your fears to the surface but also externalises them, allowing you to take action. I've found that "physically" destroying my fears by writing them down and then tearing up or burning the paper can be cathartic. This method has helped me become aware of my fears, particularly my fear of not being good enough and not being the best mother.

Next, identify the worst-case scenario and unpack the "what-ifs." It's usually not as horrible as we think. Do you worry that a new career may not succeed? Even if it didn't work out, what would happen? You'd find work elsewhere. You would go on. You would survive. Are you afraid of running out of money? If that happened, what would you do? You'd cut back on expenses, find joy in simpler things, or seek temporary assistance from friends or family. You would find a way to survive.

Facing fear and working towards a goal in life can be scary and stressful. I have found it helpful to begin modestly. Take a single, small step—something you are confident you can accomplish and will undoubtedly succeed at. Feel proud of yourself for that achievement, and then take another small step forward.

DEVELOP THE ROADMAP TO ACHIEVE YOUR VISION

Imagine you're learning how to bake a cake. You read books, watch videos, and even attend a baking class. You know all the ingredients, their exact measurements, and the perfect baking temperature. But what if you never actually bake the cake? All that knowledge wouldn't be put to good use, right? This is what happens when we gather knowledge but don't take action.

Knowledge is like a map. It shows you where to go, but you must take steps to get there. Without action, knowledge sits there, like a dusty old map in a drawer. It doesn't help you move forward or achieve anything. To make a difference and achieve the life you want, you need to set tangible, actionable goals and give yourself a timeframe to achieve them. By taking these steps, you transform knowledge into progress and bring your vision to life.

Let's break this down into three simple steps: setting goals, making them actionable, and giving yourself a timeframe.

- **Set Tangible Goals**: Tangible goals are clear and specific. Instead of saying, "I want to get fit," say, "I want to run 5km in three months." This goal is specific and gives you something concrete to work towards. It's like saying you want to bake a chocolate cake instead of just wanting to bake something sweet. Knowing precisely what you want helps you focus your efforts.

- **Make Them Actionable**: Once you have a tangible goal, break it into smaller, actionable steps. If your goal is to run 5km, your steps include running three times a week, gradually increasing your distance, and joining a running group for motivation. These steps are like following a recipe—one step at a time, each bringing you closer to your delicious cake.

- **Set a Timeframe** : A goal without a deadline is like a race without a finish line. Setting a timeframe helps keep you accountable and motivated. If you know you want to run that 5km in three months, you'll be more likely to stick to your running schedule. Deadlines create a sense of urgency and help you stay on track.

Knowledge without action will not shift the dial. To establish momentum, set tangible, actionable goals within a timeframe to help you achieve your vision and create the life you want.

DEVELOP SUPPORT SYSTEMS

Life is full of ups and downs. Challenges are inevitable, and facing them alone can be difficult. That's why building a supportive tribe is so important. Your tribe is a group of people who are there for you, offering support, inspiration, and different perspectives when you need them most. I've been fortunate to meet the most amazing, supportive people on my journey with whom I have formed lifelong authentic relationships.

Imagine you're climbing a mountain. The journey is long and complex, but having friends by your side makes it easier. They cheer you on and rally around you when you're tired, helping you find the best path. That's what a tribe does in life. They support you when you're struggling, inspire you to keep going, and offer new perspectives you might not have considered. When we decided to move back to Singapore, my close friends helped me with the transition.

Finding your tribe starts with connecting with people who share similar interests, values, or goals. This can include friends, family, colleagues, or even online communities. Look for people who uplift you, challenge you to grow, and stand by you during tough times.

Once you've found your tribe, it's essential to maintain those relationships. This means being there for them as much as they are there for you. Show appreciation, offer support, and keep in touch regularly. Relationships are a two-way street, and building a solid tribe requires effort from both sides.

By developing support systems, you not only create a safety net for yourself during challenging times but also build a network that aligns with your values and vision for the future. This supportive tribe helps you achieve the life you want for yourself and your family, ensuring that your journey is not only successful but also fulfilling and true to your core beliefs.

Another support system I have found useful in my journey that you can develop is journalling. Here are two types of journalling that have been incredibly helpful to me:

- **Gratitude Journalling** : Journalling focused on expressing gratitude and offloading the countless thoughts running through my mind has been immensely beneficial. The brain is physically incapable of experiencing a negative emotion when experiencing gratitude. Try to practice gratitude journalling at the same time every day for three weeks, as this will help embed it as a habit. I use a 5-minute journal daily to write down three things I'm grateful for. This simple practice will shift your focus from what's going wrong to what's going right. Gratitude journalling helps you appreciate the good things in your life, no matter how small they may be. I have started doing this, and it has helped me notice and cherish the fine details that make life worthwhile.

- **Mind Dump Journalling:** Sometimes, our minds are filled with a gazillion thoughts, making it hard to focus or relax. Mind dump journalling is about writing down everything that's on your mind. This helps clear your head, reduce stress, and organise your thoughts. By getting everything out on paper, you can see things more clearly and solve your problems more effectively. It's a way to declutter your mind and create mental space for creativity and problem-solving. This practice brings clarity and helps recognise patterns in your thoughts and emotions, leading to deeper self-awareness and personal growth.

Starting a journalling practice is easy. All you need is a notebook and a pen. Here are some tips to get started:

- **Set Aside Time:** Choose a time each day to journal, whether in the morning, before bed, or during a lunch break. Consistency is key.

- **Write Freely:** Don't worry about grammar, spelling, or making sense. Just write whatever comes to mind. This is your space to express yourself without judgment.

- **Be Honest:** Journalling is for you, so be honest about your thoughts and feelings. This will help you gain deeper insights and find solutions to your challenges.
- **Reflect:** Take time to read your entries. Reflecting on your journal can help you see patterns, track your progress, and celebrate your achievements.

In my experience, pivotal life moments occur when we take a leap of faith. Moving towards the unknown creates these crucial junctures. Even when fear stares you in the face, stepping forward helps you discover yourself.

While I haven't always gotten it right, leaning on my supportive tribe and leveraging tools like journalling to clarify my thoughts, have been invaluable in the ongoing process of refining my journey for our family. So, if you are facing a pivotal moment too, I'd encourage you to reflect, embrace the unknown and take that leap. You've got this!

SUE-ANN WILSON

Taking leaps of faith to define your authentic life: Sue-Ann Wilson's purpose.

https://esys.io/s/sue-ann-wilson

Suzanne Rath
Coach and Speaker

ABOUT THE AUTHOR: SUZANNE RATH

Suzanne Rath is a dynamic Coach, Speaker and Physiotherapist dedicated to empowering women over 40 to reclaim their health and vitality. As the award-winning founder of Wellness Embodied, Suzanne is a recognised leader in her field, blending her expertise as an endurance athlete, yoga teacher, and certified health coach to offer a holistic approach to wellness. Based in Cairns City, she provides personalised Craniosacral Therapy and SomatoEmotional Release sessions, alongside online health coaching for clients across Australia and globally.

Suzanne's approach is particularly effective for addressing chronic fatigue and burnout, areas where she has developed specialized knowledge and a unique perspective. Her award-winning leadership and passion for helping others shine through in her work, whether she's guiding an individual client or leading a corporate retreat.

As a corporate retreat and workshop leader, Suzanne crafts bespoke experiences designed to inspire teams to lead healthier, more fulfilling lives. Her workshops are immersive, blending practical health strategies with rejuvenating activities to foster a culture of well-being within corporate settings.

In addition to her in-person coaching, Suzanne is a sought-after public speaker, delivering engaging keynote presentations on topics such as:

- Becoming the CEO of Your Health: Leadership lessons for a happier, healthier you.
- Fatigue to Flourishing: Overcoming the fog of tiredness to live your best life.
- Midlife Mindset: Reframing body, career, and life for a purposeful, happy, and healthy second chapter.
- True Holistic Success: Thriving from the inside out.
- Optimal Energy: Daily habits for professional and personal fulfillment.

Suzanne's passion for the ocean, outdoors, and travel infuses her life and work with energy and enthusiasm. She is committed to seeing people live their best lives, and her unique blend of skills and experiences makes her a powerful advocate for health and wellness.

Whether you're an individual looking to transform your health journey or a corporate team aiming to enhance your collective well-being, Suzanne Rath offers the guidance, expertise, and inspiration you need to succeed. Connect with her to start your journey towards a healthier, more vibrant life today.

www.suzannerath.com.au

CHAPTER 11

THRIVING FROM THE INSIDE OUT

By Suzanne Rath

Just over 40 years ago, I was born in a rush, or as Dad says, 'eager to come out and leave her mark'. My parents own a farm in Wexford, known as Ireland's 'Sunny Southeast'. They had three children after me, all boys. From a young age, I was independent and opinionated. Nana often told the story of two-year-old Suzanne offering to make everyone tea on the night of my first brother's birth. While I had strong ideas on how my life would be—from the raising of children to the freedom I would have living in a big city—I didn't know or dare to dream too big.

The pinnacle of success was living in Dublin with a good job, a house and yearly holidays. It was 1980s Ireland—nobody had any money and it was the era of, 'children should be seen and not heard'.

As children on the farm, we largely entertained ourselves, an upbringing that has added to my self-reliance and ability to be alone. If I wasn't reading or trying to rid my brothers of their pocket money through my latest 'business', I was making up stories and imaginary worlds around the farm. I couldn't wait to grow up and be free.

Aged 12, I went to a co-educational boarding school. At first, it was a novelty—being surrounded by peers 24-7 was a stark contrast to my primary school class of 4 and the few playdates which we'd had at friends' houses. But the regimented structure of boarding school wasn't for me. I was rebellious and too 'much', often in detention for minor transgressions like being out of bed after lights out.

Up until my third year, I coasted through classes with good grades. I dreamed of being a writer and was top of my English class, regularly reading my 'A' grade essays aloud. Then, a series of events made me put my creative dreams on hold. Firstly, I fell in love for the first time and the excitement of this and growing up replaced my hobbies of reading and writing.

The following year, I was displaced from my spot at the top of our English class by the new kid, Martin. Martin's family didn't own a television and he was widely described as a 'nerd' by our unkind teenage selves. Suddenly it was Martin reading his essays aloud, while my grades slipped to Bs. I decided I was no longer talented as a writer and shelved any thoughts of doing a journalism degree. When I told my parents I wanted to be a Physiotherapist, they were delighted. With some luck, hopefully I would get a job in the health board, with stability and a good government pension.

I completed an honours degree in Physiotherapy in 2006 and returned to Trinity College Dublin to study a Masters in Sports Medicine two years later. Trinity is well known for its place in the city centre of Dublin, with famous alumni and the iconic long library and 'Book of Kells'. I describe myself as a lifelong learner—marrying my interests in health and leadership to create Wellness Embodied, the business I run today.

Initially drawn to Physiotherapy due to the diversity of the profession, throughout my clinical career, I've used my creative brain as much as my scientific/ logical brain. We know there are so many aspects of a person's life which affect their health—whether it's what we eat, how we move or sleep, our beliefs and upbringing, lifestyle and more. It never made sense to me that we would just focus on a torn muscle without looking at all of the factors which contributed to it. I've always wanted to enable and inspire the person in front of me to be healthier and happier than before.

While working in my first Physiotherapy job in Waterford, I took up running. This ignited a lifelong love of endurance events and a desire to see what my body is capable of. My running friends and I often travelled to several local races a week and trained for our first marathon together. I was a pretty good club runner, but I enjoyed being fit and running in new places and events more than constantly chasing faster times.

Always looking for the next challenge, I've completed eight road marathons (including qualifying for Boston in 2014), four Half Ironman distance triathlons, as well as three ultra trail marathons. I've climbed Kilimanjaro in Africa and ran, paddle-boarded, cycled and kayaked from the island of Korcula to Dubrovnik harbour in Croatia. I'm also a PADI certified rescue and self-reliant scuba diver.

Endurance sport, for me, is solid training for life - in the course of a training block or an event, you go deep within yourself, experiencing some of the greatest lows as well as the peaks of completion and achievement. Trail-running events in particular, as well as the Rat Race multisport events which I've recently discovered with my brother, emphasise the journey, rather than just the destination. I choose to live by my values—growth and adventure—by planning events as a part of my life.

Initially, I was bored with all of my jobs after a couple of years. Having recently learnt the life changing assessment tool, 'Working Genius', I know why. My areas of genius are invention and wonder, which means I am most at ease in work that involves big-picture thinking, idea creation and problem-solving. The day-to-day work of Physiotherapy can involve a lot of repeated explanations and 'galvanising' of people to follow a treatment plan which they may or may not buy into. I just wanted people to 'do the thing!'

I was also frustrated at the lack of holistic, whole person thinking of some of my colleagues in the Medical and Allied Health fields. I still believe there's far too much emphasis on the magic scan, pill or surgery within healthcare. For six years, I moved from hospital physiotherapy work to private practice, supplementing my work with high-level sports team Physiotherapy. I also volunteered in Uganda for four months, working in a hospital with a charity wing to train local Physiotherapists and set up vital services such as exercise programs for clients with HIV. I had a constant desire to change lives—I just wasn't sure how to get there.

My next big adventure came several years after I returned from Uganda, when I followed my heart to Australia and never left! Some say a good 'meet story' predicts a successful relationship. In my mid-twenties, watching *Coldplay* on the shoulders of a cute Australian at a music festival in Dublin, then meeting up again in New Zealand and Sydney, was the perfect story to tell as I prepared to move to my new home. The relationship soon fizzled out, but I'm still here 12 years later!

Sydney was a lonely place at first, but I found my tribe and immersed myself in a life of creativity, working enough as a Physiotherapist to pay the bills. I made amateur short films with friends for Kino Sydney (and produced an award-winning short, *The Noose*). I was a theatre reviewer, too, an unpaid gig which afforded me amazing tickets for opening nights at the likes of Belvoir Street and Sydney Theatre Company, with actors such as Hugo Weaving and Cate Blanchett in regular attendance. Our group of friends were always doing something — warehouse parties in the Inner West, exhibition openings, gigs and more. It was fantastic — until one day, it wasn't.

On Thursday, 31st October 2013, I was cycling along McEvoy Street in Alexandria, on my way home from one of my three Physiotherapy jobs. It was a sunny afternoon and I was excited — that night was the Newtown Hotel's birthday party and The Preatures were playing a free gig. As I wheeled slowly downhill through a green light, I spotted a car traveling in the opposite direction to me and the driver turned right across my path.

I braked, hard. Time turned to milliseconds as I registered her slowing and realised she wasn't going to make the corner. I hit the rear passenger side of her car first with my bike, then my face, as I flew over the handlebars. She stopped, as did several onlookers. My teeth hurt and felt loose; my shoulder and knee were bleeding. All I wanted was to be cleared to go home so I could make the gig. The looks on the paramedics' faces soon told me this wouldn't be happening.

Hours passed in the emergency department. I had an open fracture of my chin, multiple fractures of the right side of my jaw and a fractured external auditory canal. I was discharged at 11pm, to await surgery 'when we call you'.

I kicked into planning mode — buying lots of fresh fruits and vegetables, making soups. As far as I was concerned, I'd have a couple of weeks off work, get some writing done and everything would be fine. Five days later, I had surgery to apply arch bars to my top and bottom teeth, effectively splinting my teeth together to allow the bones to heal. All seemed fine, until the anaesthetic and painkillers wore off.

At 3am, I texted my then-boyfriend, begging him to come and get me as soon as he could—and to bring dental wax. The arch bars had tiny hooks sticking out from my gums, which were grating against the back of my lips and causing excruciating mouth ulcers. I couldn't speak and the only liquids I could consume were those which would fit behind my back teeth. Back in our Newtown terrace, the difficult healing journey was about to begin and would be far slower than I'd imagined.

Back home, I couldn't sleep, had constant pain in my face and head and lacked the concentration or focus to read a book, let alone to write. When my housemates went to work, I would alternate between pacing the house and lying around in a depressed lethargy, unable to find joy in anything. There were many friends who promised to visit and bring soup—and few who actually did.

When visitors did come, I was easily exhausted and could sense their impatience as they waited for me to answer questions by writing on a whiteboard. Several weeks after the initial surgery, the elastics holding my teeth together were released and I could talk a little, but the pain and my mental health struggles continued. Our friends were starting to turn thirty and I barely tolerated birthday dinners and parties. I was noise-sensitive, always exhausted and unable to focus on a conversation when others were talking around me.

Seven weeks after the initial surgery, on Friday the 13th, Dr Rizk (yes—it's pronounced 'risk'. And no, I'm not superstitious!), removed the arch bars and I was discharged. I quickly realised I didn't have the mental capacity to work as a private practice Physiotherapist, so I kept only one of my jobs—an easy rehab role for three days a week. Even at that, I regularly came home from work and got into bed at 5pm. My boyfriend and I argued all the time about everything. My lack of 'fun' and his unequal carrying of the household load were regular themes. A year after the accident, I still wasn't 'better', and we broke up.

I talked about 'before' and 'after' the accident. I 'used to be able to run', I 'used to be fun', I 'used to have energy'. I had chronic fatigue and constant pain and anxiety, yet I had to drive my own healing journey and find the right professionals to help me. I saw a psychologist, several physiotherapists, a massage therapist, and a top integrative doctor. Diagnoses came, unaccompanied by clear treatment options: I had Chronic Inflammatory Response Syndrome (integrative doctor) and an Adjustment Disorder (psychiatrist).

I struggled on and realised a more relevant diagnosis of post-concussion syndrome, which I confirmed with my GP. I was determined life wasn't going to be like this forever. I found a physiotherapist, Louise, who solely practices Craniosacral therapy, which brought me the extra 20% improvement in my pain and tension I'd been seeking for so long. Slowly, with time, patience and treatment, I was improving and it was time to re-evaluate my life.

I was single, with no savings and a part time job in an expensive city, as well as an ongoing battle with the insurers of the driver to pay for my medical bills and time off work. It was time to leave Sydney.

In August 2015, I packed a rented campervan to the hilt with my belongings and my puppy Banksy and we drove down King Street, Newtown to start the long drive to the Northern Territory. I'd accepted a private practice role in Katherine, knowing I had the freedom to pick my own hours and manage my day. It was the perfect chance to return to the parts of Physiotherapy I knew so well, without the stress of Sydney hours and commutes.

When I arrived in Katherine, I felt as if I'd landed in the 'real Australia'. I spent 18 months working in town and Indigenous communities, visiting places that are unseen by many who pass through, swimming in beautiful waterholes and watching stunning sunrises and sunsets. As a coastal girl, it was never going to be a forever place for me, but the time I spent there was rich with cultural experiences, connection and healing.

In Katherine I could practice Physiotherapy how I wanted, a privilege not always afforded in the workplace. But I'm only one person and I knew that to make a more impactful difference to each individual, as well as a larger volume of society, I needed a team. My experience after my accident, where I needed to seek out the right health professionals for me, taught me both the importance of a multidisciplinary team and how exhausting it is for patients to put that support network together for themselves.

In 2017, I moved to Cairns and set up Wellness Embodied as a sole practitioner in a single rented room. Business was slow at the start—I knew nobody in Cairns and worked hard to build a network and caseload. 7 years later, my vision of a multi-disciplinary practice has been realised, with three clinics in Cairns and one in Cooktown.

Outwardly, I'm successful—a self-made and driven business woman with multiple clinics. Wellness Embodied has grown exponentially since 2020, expanding to the full team of Allied Health Professionals I'd envisioned, treating both the body and mind. There's been steep learning curves—the pain of having my trust in team members broken, countless stressors and sleepless nights, creating a business which wasn't set to scale efficiently—to name a few!

There's also been recognition: Winning the 2023 Cairns Businesswoman of the Year award and the 2021 Excellence in

People Management Award (BEX/ Cairns Chamber of Commerce), finalist in the 2022 Queensland Telstra Awards, the 2021 Customer Service BEX awards & the 2019 Cairns Business Women's Club awards (Small Business Owner). I have great pride in our leadership and clinical team and the amazing service we deliver, the reviews we get, the donations we make and the volunteering and education we do within the community. We're innovative and always growing our offerings to assist our clients. We've recently opened Cairns Hyperbaric Oxygen Therapy, becoming the first space in Cairns to offer mild hyperbaric oxygen therapy, which has amazing results for inflammation reduction and improvement of chronic health concerns.

Yet the success I've achieved is more about how I feel inside. It's simple to define, yet requires strong boundaries and deep inner work to attain and keep. Success is knowing my values and living an intentional and full life according to these. It's staying healthy, growing in both body and mind, to be an active participant in all stages of life. Success requires taking responsibility for myself and my own journey of health and wellbeing.

That's not always easy to do. Fritz Perls, one of the founding fathers of Gestalt therapy, has some amazing quotes about change. He tells us that, no matter how uncomfortable our situations and the desire to escape them, our opposing pull to maintain the status quo is equally as powerful—no matter how painful the status quo may be. We may want to be healthier, to travel more, or to chase our dreams, but our beliefs and conditioning limit us. 'It's genetic, I'm too old, I'm not strong enough, I don't have time,' are some of the regular comments I hear from people when it comes to why they can't do as much as they say they would like to.

Unfortunately, we can only fully progress when we take full ownership of our own journey!

After my jaw fracture, when I first went for Craniosacral Therapy, I had a vague idea of what Louise was doing physically to 'fix' me. For me, it seemed to work and the relief lasted for a longer period of time than massage or many other modalities had. Then, she started to ask me questions—about what was happening in my heart, or the imagery that was coming up in my body. I honestly just wanted to feel better—I wasn't there to talk and do the work!

As I recovered, I started to study the Upledger Craniosacral Therapy curriculum, moving through the core courses into somato-emotional release, immune response and more. Now, I embrace the paradigm that, as therapists, we're not fixers—we're facilitators. Sure, a pill or a surgery will help and are often necessary for our health, but why do we put so much of the power for our own well-being solely in the hands of others? The more I tune into myself, explore treatments, reflect on the health of my body and mind, do yoga, get coached and evaluate my life and habits, the easier it is for me to be aware of what I need to live a fulfilled life and act on it. And I emphasise the FULL in fulfilled.

Many people allow themselves to be fully shaped by their upbringing, or by events that 'happen to them.' Yet these events are only a piece of who we are. Today, my parents wonder with bemusement 'where they got me from'. In the past year alone, with my husband, we've swum with humpback whales in Tonga, manatees in Florida and dived with more hammerhead sharks than I could ever have dreamed of in the Galapagos. We've cycled down a volcano in Ecuador, from Cairns to Cooktown and to the Northernmost tip of Australia. We've held 6-month-old Tasmanian devils at Aussie Ark and attended our first Bluefest music festival since 2019.

I've run for longer than ever before in one day (just under 70km at Smurf's Backyard Ultra in Cairns, in case you were wondering). I've volunteered regularly with the Reef Restoration Foundation in Cairns, helping to replenish our coral nurseries with spawning coral for the future of the Great Barrier Reef. I've donated 10% of my personal income and 10% of business profits to charities which can make the most difference, engaging our team to choose their own local causes to which Wellness Embodied donates on their behalf. I've acquired and opened 2 new clinics. I've done weeks of professional development courses and coaching.

Would I have imagined any of this as a girl growing up in Ireland, with a not-very-invisible glass ceiling? Definitely not! I'm healthier and can do more than I could ever imagine — while constantly reviewing my life, habits and priorities, to ensure I live according to my values and purpose.

Fritz Perls says, "You are never too old to set another goal or to dream another dream." Yet, all too often, I see women of my age and older who give up on their dreams or don't even know what these dreams are. Whether this is due to changes in health or the pressures of modern-day living, I'm here to give you permission to look after yourself first. Permission to pursue extravagant goals because they light you up inside, while trusting that you and your body are more capable than you could ever imagine.

If you want to be the CEO of your own life, optimising your energy for health and happiness and embracing a second half full of purpose, I'm here for you! As a coach, speaker and retreat facilitator, my passion is to inspire you to connect to your body more, to build a supportive health team around you and aim for an optimised, purposeful and healthy life in this second chapter of your life. No matter what your life circumstances are, I can help you to reframe them in a more empowering way, and help you to use your skills and passion to make positive changes and become truly successful, both inside and out.

SUZANNE RATH

Coach and Speaker

https://esys.io/s/suzanne-rath

EPILOGUE

As we reach the end of "She Built It: Stories and Strategies for Women in Business," I hope you find yourself filled with inspiration, hope, and a renewed sense of purpose. The women whose stories fill these pages have faced seemingly insurmountable challenges, yet they have risen above them with grace, strength, and unwavering determination. Their journeys are not just tales of personal triumphs but beacons of possibility for every woman who dares to dream.

In our pursuit of success and fulfilment, we often face moments of doubt and uncertainty. There are times when the path ahead seems obscured by obstacles, and the beauty of our dreams feels distant and unattainable. When you experience these moments, remember the power of vision—not just our own, but the vision that others hold for us.

Seeing Beyond the Horizon

Sometimes, we are too close to our struggles to see the full picture of our potential. The daily grind, the setbacks, and the societal expectations can cloud our vision, making it difficult to see the beauty and worth of our dreams. But just because we cannot see it does not mean it isn't there. In these moments, let the belief of others in you be your lifeline.

The women in this book are living proof that sometimes we need someone else to hold that vision for us. When Michelle Huntington faced the barriers of a male-dominated industry, it was the support and belief of her mentors that helped her soar. Polina Kesov found strength in the unwavering support of her friends, who believed in her ability to lead her business to new heights despite the odds.

The Power of Belief

Belief is a powerful force. It can ignite the spark of potential within us, pushing us to achieve what we once thought impossible. Heather Disher's transformation from a bullied near-death victim to a successful businesswoman is a testament to the power of believing in oneself. Yet, her journey also highlights the importance of those who believed in her when she could not.

As women, we must lift each other up. Jo Cooper's landmark victory in the Supreme Court was not just a personal triumph but a win for every woman who has ever faced injustice. Her courage was bolstered by the collective belief in the cause she was fighting for. Sue-Anne Wilson's mission to help parents stemmed from her own traumatic experiences, but it was the belief in the power of her story that propelled her to create meaningful change.

Harnessing Our Inner Strength

Each story in this book underscores the resilience and ingenuity of women who have turned adversity into opportunity. Suzanne Rath's journey from a devastating biking accident to becoming a health advocate demonstrates how personal tragedy can inspire profound change. Her story is a reminder that our inner strength often lies dormant, waiting for the right moment to be unleashed.

Rachel Wing Man, Sophie Firmager, and Jenny Godfrey's journeys all illustrate how embracing our unique challenges can lead to incredible success. Rachel turned a disfiguring skin condition into a beauty empire, Sophie transformed corporate success into a mission to help others, and Jenny built a marketing powerhouse from her life experiences. Their stories show that our greatest strengths often emerge from our deepest struggles.

Holding the Vision for Each Other

One of the most powerful lessons we can learn is that we do not have to walk this path alone. Cristina Santangelo's pivot from a miserable corporate career to helping women shine was made possible by those who held the vision of her potential when she could not see it herself. This is the essence of community and support – holding the vision for each other when the way forward seems unclear.

In my own journey, as a sole parent who faced the unimaginable loss of my son's father, I found strength in the belief of those around me. When I tracked down an online scammer to reclaim what was stolen, it was the collective belief in my resilience that kept me going. My story, like the others in this book, is a testament to the power of having others hold the vision for us.

Pursue Your Dreams

To every woman reading this book, know that you are not alone. Each story within these pages is a thread in the tapestry of our collective strength and resilience. We believe in you. The women who have shared their journeys in this book believe in you. Your dreams are worth pursuing, and your potential is boundless.

Sometimes, you may not see the beauty of your dreams or your worth. In those moments, let the stories in this book be a reminder that your vision is valid, and your dreams are achievable. Surround yourself with those who believe in you, and let their vision of your potential light the way.

A Call to Action

As you close this book, I encourage you to take the lessons, strategies, and inspirations from these stories and apply them to your own journey. Believe in yourself, even when it seems difficult. Pursue your dreams with passion and determination. And most importantly, hold the vision for other women around you. Together, we can create a world where every woman has the support and belief she needs to achieve her fullest potential.

In closing, remember that the journey to success is not a solitary one. It is paved with the support, belief, and encouragement of those who walk alongside us. Embrace the power of vision, both yours and that of others, and let it guide you to the realisation of your dreams.

Thank you for joining us on this journey. Let's continue to celebrate and uplift each other, and in doing so, inspire the next generation of trailblazers.

With unwavering belief in your potential,

Angela Sedran

GLOSSARY

A

Adversity: Refers to the difficulties and challenges faced by individuals, which are overcome through resilience and determination.

Adventure: Describes the various exciting and challenging experiences undertaken by the individuals in their personal and professional journeys.

Apartheid: A system of institutionalized racial segregation and discrimination in South Africa that impacted the life and experiences of some contributors.

Authentic Leaders: Leaders who are genuine, transparent, and ethical, inspiring trust and motivation in others.

Australian Graduate School of Management: An institution mentioned for its role in providing advanced business education to some contributors.

B

Business Growth Accelerator: A program or service focused on helping businesses expand and achieve higher levels of success through strategic planning and execution.

BCom (Bachelor of Commerce): An undergraduate degree in commerce and business management, highlighting educational qualifications.

BHP Billiton: A global resources company mentioned in the context of professional experiences and corporate careers.

Brainz Magazine: A publication where contributors have shared insights and articles, showcasing their expertise.

Business Networks: Professional groups and associations that provide support, opportunities, and connections for business growth and development.

Bullying: The act of intimidating or mistreating someone weaker or perceived as vulnerable, discussed in the context of personal experiences.

C

Career Transition: The process of changing from one career path to another, often involving significant personal and professional growth.

Coaching: The practice of providing guidance, support, and feedback to help individuals improve their skills, achieve goals, and overcome challenges.

Community Building: Efforts to create supportive networks and communities that foster collaboration, support, and mutual growth.

Concept Designs & Marketing: A company specializing in digital marketing strategies and services, highlighting innovative business practices.

Corporate Strategy Conferences: Events where business leaders and professionals gather to discuss and develop strategies for organizational growth and success.

Core Values: Fundamental beliefs and principles that guide individuals' actions and decisions, ensuring alignment with their personal and professional goals.

Cultural Shock: The feeling of disorientation experienced when encountering an unfamiliar culture or environment, often discussed in the context of personal adaptation and growth.

D

Dedication: A section where the authors dedicate their work to specific individuals or groups who have inspired or supported them.

Determination: The quality of being persistent and resolute in achieving goals despite challenges and setbacks.

DiSC: A personality assessment tool used to understand and improve communication, teamwork, and leadership based on four personality traits: Dominance, Influence, Steadiness, and Conscientiousness.

Digital Skills: Competencies related to using digital technologies, essential for modern business practices and personal development.

Dynamic Public Speaker: A person who effectively engages and inspires audiences through compelling presentations and speeches.

E

Emotional Resilience: The ability to adapt to and recover from stressful or challenging situations, maintaining emotional well-being and stability.

Empowerment: The process of enabling individuals to take control of their lives, make decisions, and achieve their full potential.

Entrepreneurial Spirit: The drive and motivation to create, develop, and manage new business ventures, often involving innovation and risk-taking.

Executive Coach: A professional who provides guidance and support to leaders and executives to enhance their performance, leadership skills, and career development.

Extended DiSC: An advanced version of the DiSC personality assessment that provides deeper insights into individual behaviors and tendencies.

F

Family Fun Planner: An initiative or resource designed to help families plan and enjoy activities together, fostering bonding and creating positive memories.

Financial Success: Achieving monetary stability and growth through effective management, strategic planning, and successful business ventures.

Flexibility: The ability to adapt to changing circumstances and environments, essential for personal and professional growth.

Five Languages: Refers to multilingual proficiency, indicating the ability to communicate in multiple languages and understand diverse cultures.

G

Graduate School of Management: An institution that provides advanced education in business and management, mentioned for its role in the professional development of contributors.

Gratitude Mindset: A perspective that focuses on appreciating and recognizing the positive aspects of life, contributing to personal well-being and happiness.

Government Change in South Africa: Refers to the political transition post-apartheid, impacting the lives and experiences of individuals in the country.

H

Healthy Body: Emphasizes the importance of physical health and well-being, achieved through proper nutrition, exercise, and self-care practices.

Happy Mind: Focuses on mental and emotional well-being, achieved through positive thinking, mindfulness, and self-reflection.

Holistic Wellness: An approach to health that considers the whole person, including physical, mental, emotional, and social well-being.

Hong Kong: A significant location in the personal history of one of the contributors, relevant to their cultural background and experiences.

I

Inclusive Beauty: An approach to beauty that embraces diversity and promotes self-acceptance, rejecting narrow standards of beauty.

Industry Thought Leader: An individual recognized as an expert and influencer in their field, contributing innovative ideas and insights.

Intrepid Adventurer: Describes individuals who undertake bold and daring activities, often facing and overcoming significant challenges.

IT Background: Refers to the expertise and experience in information technology, relevant to modern business practices and personal skills.

J

Journaling: The practice of writing down thoughts, experiences, and reflections, used as a tool for personal growth and self-discovery.

K

King Sandwiches: An entrepreneurial venture started by one of the contributors, highlighting their journey in the food industry.

L

Leadership and Business Growth Strategies: Techniques and practices aimed at enhancing leadership skills and achieving business expansion and success.

M

Malshi Companion: Refers to a pet that provides emotional support and companionship, significant in the personal life of a contributor.

Mandela's Government: The post-apartheid government in South Africa, representing significant political and social change.

Management Consultant: A professional who provides strategic advice and solutions to businesses to improve their performance and operations.

Multimedia and Arts Degree: An academic qualification in creative fields, indicating a background in visual and performing arts, design, and media.

N

National Revenues: Refers to the financial achievements of businesses, particularly those that have reached top revenue levels in their industry.

Neuro-Linguistic Programming (NLP): A psychological approach that explores the connections between neurological processes, language, and behavioral patterns, used for personal development and communication enhancement.

Nonna (Italian Grandmother): A significant figure in the personal life of one of the contributors, providing emotional support and cultural heritage.

P

Passion: A strong enthusiasm or dedication to a particular cause, activity, or goal, driving individuals to achieve success.

PBL Group: A company mentioned in the context of professional experiences and corporate careers.

PORES X: A skincare initiative focused on making skincare accessible and effective for all, started by one of the contributors.

Positive Psychology: A branch of psychology that studies the positive aspects of human life, such as happiness, well-being, and flourishing.

Psychology Research: Studies conducted to understand human behavior, emotions, and mental processes, contributing to personal and professional development.

Public Speaking: The act of delivering speeches and presentations to an audience, highlighted as a key skill for sharing experiences and inspiring others.

R

Resilience: The ability to recover from setbacks, adapt well to change, and keep going in the face of adversity.

Retrenchment: The reduction of costs or spending in response to economic difficulty, often involving job cuts or scaling back business operations.

S

Self-Reflection: The process of introspection and examining one's own thoughts, feelings, and behaviors to gain self-awareness and personal growth.

Single Mother: Refers to the challenges and experiences of raising children alone, a theme discussed by some contributors.

Skincare Routines: Practices and habits related to maintaining healthy skin, emphasized as part of overall wellness.

Strategy Director: A professional role focused on developing and implementing strategic plans for business growth and success.

Supportive Community: Networks and groups that provide emotional, social, and professional support to individuals.

Supreme Court: The highest judicial court, mentioned in the context of legal challenges and advocacy efforts.

T

Tobogganing: An adventurous activity involving sliding down a hill on a toboggan, mentioned in the context of personal experiences.

Traditional Chinese Family: Describes the cultural background and family structure of one of the contributors, influencing their values and experiences.

Transformative 12-Week Program: A structured program designed to help business owners and leaders achieve significant personal and professional growth.

Triple Happiness Coach: A title held by one of the contributors, focusing on achieving happiness through a balanced approach to health, relationships, and personal fulfillment.

INDEX

A

About the Authors
Acknowledgements
Adventure
Adversity
Angela Sedran
Angela's Story
Accounting Degree
Australian Graduate School of Management

B

Business Growth Accelerator
BCom
Brainz Magazine
Business Networks
BHP Billiton
Beauty and Wellness
Bullying

C

Corporate Career
Corporate Strategy Conferences
Coaching
Concept Designs & Marketing
Cultural Shock
Community Building
Cristina Santangelo
Core Values
Career Transition

D

Dedication
Determination
Digital Skills
DiSC
Dynamic Public Speaker

E

Executive Contributor
Executive Coach
Extended DiSC
Emotional Resilience
Entrepreneurial Spirit
Empowerment

F

Family Fun Planner
Financial Success
Flexibility
Five Languages

G

Graduate School of Management
Government Change in South Africa
Gratitude Mindset

H

Healthy Body
Happy Mind
Hong Kong
Holistic Wellness

I

Inclusive Beauty
Industry Thought Leader
Intrepid Adventurer

Introduction
IT Background

J

Jenny Godfrey
Journaling
Jo Cooper

K

King Sandwiches

L

Leadership and Business Growth Strategies

M

Malshi Companion
Management Consultant
Main Content
Mandela's Government
Michelle Huntington
Multimedia and Arts Degree

N

National Revenues
Neuro-Linguistic Programming (NLP)
Nonna (Italian Grandmother)

P

Passion
PBL Group

PORES X
Polina Kesov
Positive Psychology
Psychology Research
Public Speaking

R

Rachel Wing Man
Resilience
Retrenchment

S

Self-Reflection
Single Mother
Skincare Routines
Sophie Firmager

Strategy Director
Supportive Community
Supreme Court
Sue-Ann Wilson

T

Tobogganing
Traditional Chinese Family
Transformative 12-Week Program
Triple Happiness Coach

W

Wellness Empire
White-Water Rafting
Wonderlab

www.ingramcontent.com/pod-product-compliance
Lightning Source LLC
Chambersburg PA
CBHW070612170426
43200CB00012B/2670